LANDMARKS ON THE ROAD TO THE KINGDOM

BY

H. RAY DUNNING

"How beautiful upon the mountains are the feet of the messenger who announces peace, who brings good news, who announces salvation, who says to Zion, 'Your God reigns." Isa. 53:7

To Bob Dixon with appreciation,
H Ray Dunning

2018

An Explanatory Note

A truncated version of this work was published a few years ago by Aldersgate Press. It did not fully represent the intention I had for the work and did not experience a very wide distribution. I appreciate the willingness of the Press to publish it and their kindness to relieve me of the commitment to the contract with them so I could refocus it and make it available in a form more like I had initially envisioned. Composed of 14 chapters, it is ideally suited for a series of Sunday school lessons (with one bonus) that normally covers 13 weeks, or a series of sermons or mid-week presentations. I believe it will make available to the average person a comprehensive perspective on the Hebrew-Christian scriptures that will enable them to see the Bible in a new light as a coherent whole rather than a collection of disparate texts. It could also help explain the presence in scripture of passages that have caused some to wonder why they are in the Bible. In a word, it implicitly embodies what I have come to believe about the nature of scripture.

Our trek through the Old Testament will demonstrate that the land plays a major role, not only in the text but also in Israel's life and self-understanding. This fact, for various reasons, has been a significant factor in the dominance of a particular emphasis among many evangelical Christians who seek to take the Bible seriously. Unfortunately, those who subscribe to this view have failed to also take seriously the transformation of perspective about the land that took place with Jesus as the Jewish Messiah. Because of this I have added, in this work, a short appendix addressing that issue, even though it often has a divisive effect among bible believing Christians.

I have imitated the pattern of the *Interpreters' Bible Commentary* (both editions) by adding a section of "Reflections" after the exegetical and theological analysis of the revelatory event. I have also reinserted the footnote documentation that was eliminated in the above mentioned version. I see this to be very important.

TABLE OF CONTENTS

Foreword

Chapter 1 – Mount Ararat – Revelation of Sin, Judgment and Mercy . . 6

Chapter 2 – Mount Moriah – Revelation of the Faithfulness of God . . 16

Chapter 3 - Mount Sinai – Revelation of the Holiness of God 28

Chapter 4 – Mounts Ebal & Gerizim – Revelation of Covenant Renewal . . 41

Chapter 5 – Mount Zion – Revelation of the Presence of God 53

Chapter 6 – Mount Carmel – Revelation of the Sovereignty of God . . 66

Chapter 7 – Mount of Vision – Revelation of the End of Exile 74

Chapter 8 – The Stone that became a Mountain 83

Chapter 9 – Sermon on the Mount – Revelation of the Kingdom of God 91

Chapter 10 – Mount of Olives – Revelation of the Vindication of Christ 102

Chapter 11 – Mount Tabor – Revelation of the Glory of Christ 112

Chapter 12 – Mount Golgotha – Revelation of the Power of Love . . .122

Chapter 13 – Mount of the Ascension – Revelation of the Rule of Christ . . .131

Chapter 14 – Mount of Final Vision – Revelation of the New Creation 145

Conclusion 155

Appendix – The Land 159

FOREWORD

When Saul of Tarsus encountered the resurrected Jesus on the Damascus Road, his entire world view was transformed. As a devout Jew, and a zealous Pharisee, he knew exactly what God was about and how that purpose was to take place. Like most devout Jews of that period he shared the belief that Israel was continuing to live in exile. Although the Babylonian Captivity had come to an end physically with the Persian conquest of the Babylonians and the rise of Cyrus the Great with many Jews returning to the homeland, they were now under the dominion of the pagan power of Rome. Theologically, the exile had never ended. "Israel had not been restored. Zechariah's ten men had not taken hold of the skirt of a Jew saying 'we will go with you, for we have heard that God is with you' (Zechariah 8:23); nor had YHWH taken his stand on Mount Zion to defeat all the nations that oppose Jerusalem (Zechariah 14:1-5). Ezekiel's new Temple had not been built, with rivers of healing water flowing out to make even the Dead Sea fresh (Ezekiel 47). And, towering over them all, Isaiah's vision of comfort, forgiveness, peace and prosperity had never been remotely near fulfillment (Isaiah 40-55)."[1] As a Pharisee of the Pharisees Saul shared the conviction that the kingdom of God would come with the overthrow of Rome.

In the light of this situation the Book of Daniel was a popular writing among Second Temple Jews.[2] And the rabbis had little difficulty identifying Rome with the fourth kingdom of Nebuchadnezzar's vision of powers that hold sway over the earth (2:36-45). The central thrust of Daniel was a call to be faithful to one's Jewishness in the face of pagan oppression. The challenge was informed by the optimism that the Kingdom of God would ultimately prevail. This faith is graphically depicted in the stone cut without hands out of the MOUNTAIN (vv. 34-35) that smote the image and broke it. This stone is the Kingdom of God that became a great MOUNTAIN.

---

[1] N. T. Wright, *What Saint Paul Really Said* (Cincinnati: Forward Movement Publications, 1997), 30.

[2] While the stories of Daniel are told of a figure who lived in the Babylonian exile, it is generally agreed among scholars that the book of Daniel in its present form belongs in the days of the persecution of Antiochus Epiphanes, mid-second century B.C.

It was the belief of the Pharisees that the realization of the Kingdom of God would be facilitated by Israel's strictly keeping the Torah, particular the purity laws. As a Shammai Pharisee, Paul intended to hasten that day by forcing other Jews to keep the Torah in this way, using violence as and when necessary. That was the meaning of "zeal" as he applied it to himself (Philippians 3:6). It was on the basis of this commitment that he obtained the authority from the chief priests to go to Damascus to seize Christians and drag them off to prison. In his view they were renegade Jews, leading Israel astray from true loyalty to the one true God.[3]

That the Kingdom of God could become reality through one who was careless about those rules and who had gathered a group of people who were negligible about those purity requirements and were critical of the Temple was unacceptable. The claim that one who had been put to death by the Romans instead of conquering them could be the Davidic Messiah was beyond his comprehension. The anomaly of these early Christian claims was exacerbated by the fact that the law in Deuteronomy had declared anyone who had died on a tree (crucifixion) to be under the curse of God (Deut. 21:23). The encounter with the risen Jesus caused him to see that contrary to all his expectations, the hope of the rule of God had reached its climax with Jesus of Nazareth and consequently his whole perspective must be reoriented. That is the point of his often-misunderstood statement in 2 Corinthians 5:16-17.

In introducing himself to the Romans Paul sums up his perspective in Romans 1:1-4—"Paul a servant of Christ Jesus, called to be an apostle and set apart for the gospel of God—the gospel he promised beforehand through his prophets in the Holy Scriptures regarding his Son, who as to his earthly life was a descendant of David, and who through the Spirit of holiness was appointed the Son of God in power by his resurrection from the dead: Jesus Christ our Lord."[4]

This analysis implies that the way Saul of Tarsus read the scriptures was as a long story that was on the way to a climax when God would put everything right. It was a story in search of an ending and he believed his own task was to bring that ending about. When he referred to that consummation as "according to the scriptures" (I Corinthians 15:1-3) he was not talking about the fulfillment of isolated texts that

---

[3]Wright, *Paul*, 35.
[4]It is important to note in this and elsewhere in Paul that "Christ" is not a proper name but should be rendered as Messiah.

predicted specific events, he was referring to the consummation of the story taken as a whole.

Scholars have searched in vain for passages that explicitly predict anything resembling a crucified and resurrected Messiah. Contrary to popular ideas, Isaiah 53 is not a messianic description, nor was it ever understood as such by Israelites. But prophetic preaching uniformly reflected the pattern of judgment in the form of exile followed by restoration and when we recognize that, for Paul, Jesus is actually Israel in one person, and that pattern is replicated by his death and resurrection that brings the exile to an end and launches the new age, we can clearly see the thrust of his claim for fulfillment of the biblical story in the Christ event.

This further means that, rightly understood, eschatology stands at the heart of a biblical theology in both testaments. Paul recognized that even though the resurrection had validated the claim that Jesus' death and resurrection had inaugurated the "age to come," the "present age" continued on. Thus, the two ages overlapped and Paul and ourselves are living in the middle, in the "time between the times." There were landmarks throughout the Old Testament that pointed forward to the consummation of Israel's story and these took place in a series of revelatory events that took place at various mountains. In like fashion we now look forward to the consummation of the Kingdom. From this perspective we have "landmarks" in the New Testament that both point to the nature of the inaugurated kingdom and also to the way forward. These too occur at mountain sites. Hence, we follow the marked-out trail from promise to fulfillment, from inauguration to consummation.

This brief description throws a brilliant light on the Hebrew Christian Scriptures, what they are about and how they are to be interpreted. These questions have exercised the minds of Christians from the beginning of the Christian era. They have usually been explored under the rubric of "authority and inspiration." The major problem with this way of framing the questions, as I see it, is that it focuses the discussion on the text(s) of scripture, rather than on its all-encompassing message. On the extreme right of the spectrum of opinion is the attempt to maintain the authority of the text by claiming that it is inerrant. In contrast, the extreme left end of the spectrum focuses on the "errancy" of the text. They are both primarily focused on the text, but the former more particularly ends up turning the Bible into something other than what it *is*. Simply put, I am suggesting that while the text is important, taken in terms of what it *is*, the Bible is the story of God. As N.T.

Wright summarily elaborates it, it is "a story about a creator and his creation, about humans made in this creator's image and given tasks to perform, about the rebellion of humans and the dissonance of creation at every level, and particularly about the creator's acting, through Israel and climactically through Jesus, to rescue his creation from its ensuing plight. The story continues with the creator acting by his own spirit within the world to bring it towards the restoration which is his intended goal for it."[5] The variations in telling the story such as textual diversity, even historical errors, or outmoded scientific concepts that may be present in the text do not touch the essential veracity of the message.

I would go a step further and suggest that behind the story and informative of its nature are theological understandings constituting a normative theological perspective. This perspective comes more fully to expression in some passages than others. In fact, it may be so negligible in some that it is virtually absent. Even the average bible reader will recognize this fact and wonder, at times, why certain passages are even in holy writ. In anticipation of what I am attempting to do in this book, it should be noted that the major revelatory moments in the Old Testament we shall be exploring in this study both anticipate and provide the theological framework[6] for the full realization of the salvation history in the Christ event and its consequences.

The biblical story thus understood is much like a safari through a strange land in search of a destination of eternal significance. In the original trek, a pioneer has found his/her way through the uncharted wilderness and prepared a map for those that follow, a map that identified landmarks that point the way to the destination. The most obvious landmark would be a highly visible object that could be seen from a distance, such as a mountain. That is actually what we have in

---

[5]*The New Testament and the People of God* (Minneapolis: Fortress Press, 1992), 132. Hoo-Jung Lee argues that the mature John Wesley came to emphasize "the *grand scheme* of redemption that embraced the whole drama of God's creation, the Fall of humanity, and the far superior New Creation," thus substantially expressing the same world view. "The Doctrine of New Creation in the Theology of John Wesley," Ph.D. dissertation, Emory University, 1991, 53.

[6]This statement has far reaching implications for the relation between the Testaments. I have spelled this out elsewhere (*Grace, Faith and Holiness*, Appendix 2) and it is extensively developed by John Bright, *The Authority of the Old Testament* (Nashville, Abingdon Press, 1967). Briefly stated it is the understanding that the relation between Old and New is theological in nature, i.e. the theology of the Old is "filled full" by that of the New. That is, the theology of the Old Testament is now given a Christological content while the formal structure of the Old remains the same.

scripture. Crucial, formative theological landmarks on the journey to the consummation are identified as occurring at certain mountains where formative theological truths come to expression. In fact, a careful study of these mountain revelations can provide a sketchy but comprehensive and coherent picture of biblical theology and help us grasp the normative understanding of biblical faith.

Chapter One

MOUNT ARARAT

Revelation of Sin, Judgment, and Mercy

But God remembered Noah and all the wild animals and all the domestic animals that were with him in the ark. And God made a wind blow over the earth, and the waters subsided; the fountains of the deep and the windows of the heavens were closed, the rain from the heavens was restrained, and the waters gradually receded from the earth. At the end of one hundred fifty days, the waters had abated; and in the seventh month, on the seventeenth day of the month, the ark came to rest on **the mountains of Ararat** (Gen. 8:1-4).[7]

Mountains of Arafat

The story of Noah's Ark is one of the most familiar and often told events recorded in the Bible. It has captured the imagination of children for generations. It has been the source of adventure tales for moviemakers. It has even been used by Fundamentalists as evidence for the theory that the earth is only a few thousand years old. Its most important and evidently divinely intended theological function, however, is the role it serves in Genesis 1-11. These eleven chapters tell the story of the human race. They identify the need and lay the foundation for the story of

---

[7]Unless otherwise indicated scripture references in this work are from the New Revised Standard Version.

God's activity directed toward the restoration of his fallen creation. This story begins with the call of Abraham in Genesis 12.

The Need for a New Creation

The first two chapters of the Book of Genesis introduce the reader to God the Creator. One purpose of these chapters is to let us know that the origin of the "heavens and the earth" as we know it is not the result of blind random forces. As the narrative pictures the Lord God bringing an ordered universe into being out of primeval "chaos," (Genesis 1:1—2:1a) we are to learn that we are inhabitants of a realm that was created with a purpose. For this reason, the Creator declared it to be "good," a purpose word. The climactic act of this ordered realm was the bringing into being of two human beings who bore the image of the Creator.

Because of their image bearingness, human beings were to be the stewards of the remainder of the creation and thus serve as vice-regents of the Lord God. The secret to their happiness and a meaningful existence was maintaining a proper relation to the Creator. This relation was to be maintained by communion with the Creator and observance of the one prohibition imposed on them: they were not to eat of the "tree of the knowledge of good and evil." (Gen. 2:17).

Unfortunately, both for them and for their descendents, they chose to ignore the warning about the consequences of eating the forbidden fruit. By assuming that they knew more than the Sovereign about what was good for them, they chose to be their own gods. According to Genesis 1-11 this tragic decision began a tale of woe that seemed to become worse and worse as time wore on. The situation eventually reached such a dreadful state that the Creator felt sorrow that he had initiated this project. In the original creation, as noted above, God had brought order out of chaos but the corruption of the creation was so advanced that it appeared to be returning to chaos. The Creator had two options, either completely put an end to the project or begin again. In love and mercy, he decided to begin again. Following the inevitable judgment on the corrupt world that took place in the form of a massive flood, the subsiding of the floodwaters and the landing of the ark on the top of Mount Ararat signaled the beginning of a "new creation." Why was a new creation necessary? The answer to that question is the key point in the narrative.

Theology of the Flood

Many persons have questioned the historical validity of the universal flood as reported in Genesis 6-8. Although the Bible believer does not need supporting evidence, such confirmation is available from ancient documents. While the historical reality of the event is important, the most significant aspect of it is the theological and is the primary point the biblical writer is making.

A modern-day flood illustrates the way 21st century persons view occurrences as opposed to the view of ancient persons. In 2010, the area where I live experienced a devastating flood. I was out of the city at the time and was unable to return home for a few days because all incoming roads were totally immersed. The meteorologists of the television stations had a field day reporting the consequences of such torrential rain. Not one, however, attributed it to supernatural causes. That fact highlights the great difference between the ancient mind and the modern one. All ancient people believed that the gods caused unusual cosmic events. The contrast between the biblical explanation for the flood and that of the other contemporary ones helps us highlight the theological meaning of the great flood as described in Genesis.

According to the major non-biblical account, the gods used the flood to eliminate the human race because humankind was multiplying too much and their noise was disturbing the peace of the gods. After a mythical description of the creation, it describes the reason for the flood in this verse:

> Twelve hundred years had not yet passed
> When the land extended and the people multiplied.
> The land was bellowing like a bull,
> The god got disturbed by their uproar.
> Enlil heard their noise
> And addressed the other gods,
> "The noise of mankind has become too intense for me,
> With their uproar I am deprived of sleep.[8]

As in the Genesis story, this other account known as the Babylonian Epic includes a surviver of the flood. However, this survivor did so only because he happened to worship a crafty and powerful deity

---

[8]Quoted in David Clines, "Noah's Flood I: The Theology of the Flood Narratives," *Faith and Thought* 100.2 (1972-3), 130

who disagreed with the other gods' decision to exterminate humankind. The contrast of this explanation with the rationale for the flood reported in Genesis is striking: "The Lord saw that the wickedness of humankind was great in the earth and that every inclination of the thoughts of their hearts was only evil continually. . . . for the earth is filled with violence because of them" (Gen. 5:5, 13). Here is briefly stated the rationale for the flood. The world in which order first arose out of cosmic chaos has been reduced to moral chaos. As one writer described it, it is "chaos-come-again." What was happening in Noah's time is vividly described in Genesis 6:12—"the earth was corrupt; for all flesh had corrupted its ways upon the earth." With the whole created enterprise gone awry, it would seem just to bring a total end to the entire project. However justice is tempered with mercy and, like the whole of Genesis 1-11, the flood narrative reflects a beautiful mixture of judgment and mercy.

Signs of Mercy

In spite of the fact that justice dictated that judgment fall on the degenerate human race, the Creator's love manifested in mercy appears throughout these eleven chapters. The repeated violations of God's creative intention, which is the essence of sin (see Romans 3:23), were accompanied by announcements of judgment. Nevertheless, in every case the announced consequences were moderated by grace. Adam and Eve were warned that if they ate of the forbidden fruit they would "die." Although they were expelled from the garden, they did not die on the day they ate. According to Genesis 5, Adam lived nine hundred and thirty years. An even more dramatic evidence of mercy, which gives us an insight into the nature of God on the very threshold of human history, occurred following the eating of the forbidden fruit. According to Genesis 3:8-9, the Creator came to the regular evening tryst with the human pair *as if* nothing had happened. Did he not know? Clearly, we have a picture of a God of infinite love, not a deity that was offended, needing to be appeased. The Creator's first response was a move to restore the broken relation. This truth so clearly demonstrated at the threshold of human history has been too easily forgotten by certain theological traditions in their formulations of a theory of the Atonement.

The same pattern recurs throughout this opening section of Genesis. Though Cain was cursed, a mark was put on him to protect his life. The scattering of the people who sought to build the Tower of Babel as an expression of human arrogance was succeeded by the call of Abraham to be God's instrument to "put things right." Thus, the entire primeval history is characterized by an interplay of both justice and mercy that conveys God's intent to be redemptive and never merely retributive. This recurring pattern is reminiscent of the words of Paul, "where sin increased, grace abounded all the more" (Rom. 5:20).

In the case of the developments leading up to the Flood, the description of the sin that triggered it is found in Genesis 6:5, 11f. This description is followed by a speech of the Lord: "So the Lord said, 'I will blot out from the earth the human beings I have created—people together with the animals and creeping things and birds of the air, for I am sorry that I have made them." The expression of mercy is recorded in v. 8—"But Noah found favor in the sight of the Lord." The punishment is recorded in Genesis 7:6-24, but the destruction is not total.

The basic distortion of God's intentions for the creation had to do with the fact that humans were created in the image of God (Genesis 1:26-28). To be in God's image meant being in right relation with the Creator, to other persons and to the earth. Although the act of disobedience by the first pair primarily disrupted their relationship of communion with the Creator, that disrupted relationship also manifested itself in the disruption of human relations as well as their relationship to the soil. Every relationship that constituted humanity in the image of God was affected, and the outcome was mankind's alienation from authentic humanness. This disruption of proper relationships resulted in the emergence of grossly sub-human behavior, which was demonstrated repeatedly throughout the Old Testament. In spite of these continuing consequences of sin, scripture includes the subtle reminder again of God's grace in Genesis 9:6 where God prohibits murder because humankind is still in the image of God.

Perhaps the most poignant symbol of hope that God will not abandon the creation, but preserve it and ultimately redeem it, is the rainbow. For those who have eyes to see and hearts to understand, this beautiful image in the sky is more than refracted light through a rain drop. It is a sign that the Creator's love for his creation will finally overcome the bondage to decay and will truly bring into being a new creation. In some of the darkest moments in the history of God's people, prophets were given a vision of the throne of God surrounded by a rainbow. During the bleak days of the Babylonian captivity, Ezekiel was encouraged by it (Eze. 1:28).

At the end of the first century A.D. when the church was facing persecution with potential annihilation, John the Revelator caught a glimpse of the rainbow. Years later T.O. Chisholm, inspired by Isaiah 49:14-16, related this comforting vision of hope to personal experience in his song, "He will not forget:"

> As I journey on along life's changeful way,
> Whether in the sunshine or 'mid shadows gray.
> If with dangers threatened or by foes beset,
> Faith and hope keep singing, "He will not forget."
> He will not forget, God will not forget,
> Never hath one child been forgotten yet;
> Mothers have been known to forget their own,
> His is love unchanging, He will not forget.[9]

The New Creation

Failing to live out the Creator's intention, humanity had paved the way for the destruction of the entire creation. But God in his mercy was not willing to abandon the project: "God remembered Noah." Because of this one righteous man, creation would not be permanently undone. So Noah and his family, along with two of each species of animals, are to be saved to begin the creation all over again. Noah is picured in Genesis 9:1-9 as a "new Adam" who presides over a restored world, a renewal of creation echoing the terms and imagery of Genesis 1:26-31. The same vocation initially given to Adam is now addressed to Noah. In a real sense, because of God's persistent mercy, a "new creation" would be allowed to emerge. Perhaps it would go right this time. With the destruction of all sinners it would appear that the world was again Eden-like.

Unfortunately, it was not to be. No sooner had the waters subsided and the ark moored on the mountains of Ararat than the sad truth became apparent. Although external evil had been dealt with, there was a deeper problem that the flood had not addressed. Humankind still retained something of the image of God (Gen. 9:6), but it was obviously a distorted image in need of full restoration. The reappearance after the flood of the same situation that resulted in the judgment of the flood clearly demonstrates that there was an internal problem that could not be corrected by *external* factors. What was needed was an *internal*

---

[9]In the public domain

transformation. The remainder of the long story in the Old Testament bears vivid testimony to the truth of this fact.

How does one explain the almost unrelieved failure of a people who had been rescued from slavery? Moses declares both the cause and consequences of Israel's continuing disobedience in his farewell address as reported in Deuteronmy 28-30. He recognizes that Israel's ongoing apostasy will eventually result in their being excluded from the land and carried into captivity again. But that outcome will not be the last word! When they repent the Lord will restore them and "circumcise [their hearts] and the heart[s] of your descendents, so that you will love the Lord your God with all your heart and with all your soul, in order that you may live" (Deut. 30:6). Both Jeremiah and Ezekiel, prophesying in the context of the impending destruction of Jerusalem by Babylon, recognized that the real problem was the unconverted heart. As Jeremiah put it, "[T]he heart is devious above all else; it is perverse—who can understand it?" (Jeremiah 17:9) and announced a new covenant that would remedy the wayward heart (31:31-35). Ezekiel identified the same problem and anticipated a remedy that would provide for the needed inner transfformation (Eze. 36:25-27).

Sin and Grace

The aftermath of the flood demonstrated conclusively that solutions that address only sinful *behavior* are inadequate to deal with the human predicament. The problem lies deeper than actions; there is a problem with the "heart." While it is true that acts of sin need forgiveness, the more profound need is inner transformation. Genesis 6:5 offers one of the most devastating analyses of the human condition in all scripture: "[T]he Lord saw that the evil of man was great in the earth and that every idea of the plans of his mind was nothing but evil all the time." Few biblical texts are so explicit and all-embracing in specifying the extent of human sinfulness. This pessimistic picture is not limited to the Old Testament. The Apostle Paul draws a picture of the pagan world in Romans 1:18-32 remarkably like the picture of the pre-flood people. The pagan world, says Paul, was a cesspool of iniquity, distorting every relationship the Creator designed in his original intention. But he also emphasizes that even the moral Jew is not exempt from the source of this corruption. Identifying himself with his kinsmen by using first-person singular voice, he describes their history graphically in Romans 7:7-25.[10] Almost synonymous with the giving of the law (Torah), Israel was busy violating its first prohibition with the golden calf. The Torah, which was good, was unable to accomplish its purpose because the material with which it had to do was weak. Paul referred to this weakness as "flesh."

"Original sin," the label used by theologians, has been defined and explained in various ways, but it is the most indisputable doctrine of the Christian faith. Evidence of it is everywhere! It is the rationale for the fact, as Paul says, that "all have sinned and fall short of the glory [image] of God" (Romans 3:23). It is the explanation for the Christian conviction that human beings cannot return to the Garden of Eden by their own initiative. The implication is that no one can turn to God unless God provides the capacity to respond to his overtures of grace. This fact is the reason why the Christian faith has, with few exceptions, consistently affirmed the doctrine of "total depravity."

One of the distinctive emphases of Wesleyan theology is its belief that God has, in fact, given every human being the capacity to respond to God's saving invitation. This gracious provision of the Lord is termed "prevenient grace." The term *prevenient* means "that which goes before." It is always God's first move! Others have used the concept, but it is a centerpiece of the Wesleyan position. It is the basis for the Wesleyan belief that grace is extended universally, offering the free gift of salvation to every person everywhere. St. Paul describes prevenient grace sharply in these words: "But God proves his love for us in that while we still were sinners Christ died for us" (Romans 5:8). From the moment of the fall into sin until the consummation of history, God has extended his hand in seeking reconciliation with his alienated creation and will continue to do so. At the very end of human history, the invitation is still extended: "The Spirit and the bride say, 'Come.' And let everyone who hears say, 'Come.' And let everyone who is thirsty come. Let anyone who wishes take the water of life as a gift" (Rev. 22:17).

Scripture records that human beings, in spite of their failures, still retained something of the image of God (Gen.9:6), but it was obviously a distorted image in need of redeeming. It was to that task, again in mercy, that God set himself in the election of Abraham and his descendents. The origin and meaning of this election provide the next mountain landmark.

---

[10]Cf. N.T. Wright, "Romans" in the *New Interpreter's Bible*, vol X (Nashville: Abingdon Press, 2003),

REFLECTIONS

The narratives in Genesis 1 – 11 are not directly about individual religious experience, although they clearly have implications for such. They are addressing the predicament of the entire human race of which each of us is a representative member. The picture we see in these chapters is of a sorry mess. Like the civilization of Noah's day after the flood, humanity has consistently restarted itself with hopes that this new beginning would eliminate the evils of the past and usher in a utopia of peace and prosperity. One of the signal examples of this was the rise of the Roman Empire. Of great interest to our contemporary civilization was the hope that surrounded the ascension of a new Emperor. The Roman poet Virgil expressed that hope for the Empire in a formula: *novus ordo seclorum*, "a new world order."

After the so–called Dark Ages, the new discoveries of science and the renewed confidence in human reason and ability that marked the 18th Century Enlightenment led to the optimistic expectations that informed both the French and the American revolutions. In fact, the motto of Virgil is emblazoned on the great seal of the United States. It can be seen on the back of a one-dollar bill. How has it turned out? Do we really have a new world order of peace and harmony?

The aftermath of the flood highlights the real reason for the unending array of failed civilizations.[11] The problem is not inadequate government or weak laws; it is the internal condition of human beings. Why then, does not the human race annihilate itself? We find the clue in the Genesis narratives themselves. It is the mercy of God that tempers judgment and stands as a bulwark against total chaos and guards against complete self-annihilation. Overall, the Creator is seeking to restore his fallen creation to the glory that marked his original intention for it.

If we can sneak a peek into what the biblical story tells us after it describes the apparently hopeless plight of the human situation, we can have hope that God will eventually bring to reality a "new creation" that will transcend the attempt at a "new creation" that began with Noah and his family. It will be one in which humanity will be restored fully to the image of God and "the knowledge of the Lord will cover the earth as waters cover the sea." Quite a contrast to the flood of Noah!

---

[11] Cf. the work of historian Arnold Toynbee.

Until that final consummation, God makes available to each of us in his provision of grace through Jesus Christ the possibility of a transformation of heart so that we may become a "new creation" ourselves in anticipation of the time when heaven and earth shall come together in a "new heavens and new earth wherein dwells righteousness." Until that day, a rainbow circles over our heads and sings of love and mercy to our race.

> This Is My Fathers world
> O let me ne'er forget
> that tho' the wrong seems oft so strong,
> God is the ruler yet.
> This is my Fathers world
> the battle is not done;
> Jesus who died, shall be satisfied,
> and earth and heaven be one.
>   – – Maltbie D Babcock

Questions to Think About

1. In light of the Bible's teaching about the universality of sin, how would you explain the goodness seen in many non-Christian human beings?

2. If we take "original sin" seriously, how would you evaluate the popular evangelistic appeal to "make a decision for Christ?"

3. What do you think is the motive for God's mercy? Is it God's nature or human worth?

4. How would you evaluate the 19th century holiness movement's claim that entire sanctification eradicated original sin?

Chapter Two

Mount Moriah

Revelation of the Faithfulness of God

So Abraham called that place "The Lord will provide"; as it is said to this day, "On the mount of the Lord it shall be provided" (Genesis 22:14)

Mount Moriah

From the vantage point of Mt. Ararat, we caught a glimpse of the need of human beings to be rescued from their desperate situation resulting from the sin of Adam and Eve. We saw that even though justice indicated the necessity of judgment, that judgment was always moderated by mercy. Thus, at the threshold of the biblical story we saw that the Creator was from the beginning seeking to redeem the wayward creation. That effort took a specific direction with the call of a man from Mesopotamia named Abram, whose name was later changed to Abraham. That call was the initial expression of the biblical concept of election. It was an election to a vocation that both he and his descendents were to carry out. They were to be the means through whom God would put things right.

Abram's "call" included a three-fold promise: a land, a seed, and the assurance that he would be the means of a worldwide blessing (Genesis 12:1-3). That blessing would involve a reversal of the ancient curses in Eden that affected the earth, human relationships and stewardship of the creation. God's plan for salvation from the beginning was that "all nations shall be blessed" that is, he would reverse the curse on the entire creation through Abram and his descendents.

Abraham's Pilgrimage

Abram was a "pagan" when he first "heard" the voice of God. God apparently had to issue the call twice, once in Ur and once in Haran, but the patriarch eventually answered it. His obedient response began a long journey as the Lord brought him gradually to the maturity of faith that befitted the father of the redemptive people of God. It is evident that the culmination of that personal spiritual journey reached its climax on Mount Moriah. Abraham became known as the "father of the faithful" as the outcome of that crucial event (Hebrews 11:8f).

In evaluating Abraham's pilgrimage, it is easy to forget that he did not grow up in Sunday school. He and his family members were idolaters. According to Jewish tradition, they were more than likely star worshippers. He had no source book to consult for learning about the God who had called him to leave his country and family and follow into the unknown. Actually, there were many unknowns: the place, the outcome, and above all the nature of the God whose voice he had heard and to whom he had responded. Just as his faith matured through the years of his pilgrimage, so Abraham's comprehension of this God also matured. His experience demonstrates that there is an inseparable connection between faith and understanding. The Apostle Paul emphasized this relation when he prayed for his converts to grow in knowledge (Philippians 1:9-11).

Faith is understood biblically as response to a promise (Romans 10:17). The validity and possibility of the fulfillment of any promise is in the integrity of the one who made the promise. The Greek poet Aeschylus (c.524-c.555 B.C.) once said, "It is not the oath that makes us believe the man, but man the oath." God's promises to Abraham were originally made in Mesopotamia (Gen. 11: 27-32), but it was only on Mount Moriah that Abraham eventually came to the full realization of the faithfulness of the one he knew as El Shaddai (Gen. 17:1). His experience on Moriah enabled him to assign the title of Jehoveh-Jireh to his God, meaning, "God will provide."

In more than one experience prior to the traumatic call to sacrifice the son of promise Abraham had failed to recognize and live by faith that the God he was following would keep his promises. When he faced the threat of starvation because of a famine, he was unable to trust God's promise to provide for him in the land to which he had been led. Therefore, he departed to Egypt—with dire consequences. When the promise of a son was long delayed, he allowed himself to be persuaded by Sarai to take things into his own hands and father a child from Hagar—again with dire consequences.

The climactic event on Mount Moriah gave Abraham the final, persuasive evidence that God's word is sure and steadfast. Abraham was facing a decision with momentous consequences for the promise on which he had been building his life. The dilemma was intensified by the triple reference to "your son, your only son, the son you love." To sacrifice his son surely would end the promise in disaster, and furthermore God's integrity would be in question. If he refused, his relation to God would be endangered and he would forfeit the promised blessings. It appeared to be a no-win situation. Somehow, he must take his courage in both hands and by obedient faith trust that God would keep his promise in the face of all appearances to the contrary. By taking this dramatic leap of faith, he discovered in his obedience that both the son would be saved and the promise fulfilled.

God was evidently seeking to teach Abraham this characteristic of himself all along. This conclusion might be suggested by the fact that after this final test the narrative becomes quite uneventful. No other exciting tales about Abraham are told. Sarah dies and is buried. Abraham remarries and raises a second family and is finally laid to rest in the Promised Land. Then the story moves on! Genesis 22:16-18 implies that a barrier has been broken, that the promise can now flow not only to Abraham's family but also out into the wider world.

God's Covenant Faithfulness

The crucial event in establishing God's covenant with Abraham had occurred on Mount Moriah. God's faithfulness in keeping his promise had been nailed down there and points to the future that extends into the present day. In the light of this truth, it is important to explore the meaning of covenant. The very essence of covenant relationship is promise making and promise keeping. It is equally important to recognize the purpose of this covenant. As numerous Jewish texts make clear, God called Abraham in order that through his family he might undo the sin of Adam. This truth also stands at the heart of the theology of St. Paul as well as the rest of the New Testament.

We can trace God's faithfulness to this covenant with Abraham's descendents through the pages of the Old Testament. Far too often his faithfulness is in stark contrast to the faithlessness of Israel. The faithfulness of the Caller and faithlessness of the called crop up again and again both in prayers for the Lord to remember his wayward people and in passages of celebration giving praise to God for his faithfulness to the promises to Abraham and in later times, to David.

The term that expresses God's faithfulness to the covenant is the Hebrew word *chesed*. It defies simple translation so is rendered in various ways. The King James Version often uses "lovingkindness" which is not inaccurate but does not catch its full significance. The Revised Standard Version chose "covenant or steadfast love," which gets closer, but perhaps something like "loving loyalty to promises given" is as close to the word's real meaning as we can get. The meaning of *chesed* is similar to a wedding vow when a couple pledge their "troth" to each other and then lovingly live out that commitment.

The classic use of the concept is in the book of Hosea where the relation of Yahweh and Israel is illustrated by a marriage in which both faithfulness (*chesed*) and unfaithfulness (lack of *chesed*) are manifested respectively by the prophet and his spouse. The marriage analogy is particularly appropriate because, like the ideal marriage, the covenant is different from a contract. A contract is entered into by two parties for benefits to be derived by one or both. The goal of a covenant is intimacy and when it degenerates into a contractual arrangement, it ceases to be the relationship of communion that God intended.

There were times when it appeared that the covenant promises would come to naught because of the faithlessness of Israel. There were dark days when she was on the verge of extinction because of failure to keep covenant. God had to adjust his plan, eventually abandoning the hope that the nation as a whole would be the agent of redemption. In the time of Isaiah, he turned to a faithful remnant within the people, like Elijah's 7,000 who had not bowed the knee to Baal. Isaiah's vision of the stump that would remain when the tree (the nation) was cut down (Isaiah 6:12-13) embodied the idea of the remnant. Whatever happened, God would remain faithful to his promise to Abraham.

As implied by Isaiah's righteous remnant God's faithfulness on occasion had to make significant adaptations. One of my theology professors liked to describe God as like a "heat seeking missile" that changed its course in pursuit of its quarry. This is an apt illustration. God's faithfulness adapting to the situation is specifically recognized by

Jeremiah in his object lesson of the potter and the clay. This imagery has captured the imagination of popular piety as a picture of the sincere person compliantly yielding, like clay, to the shaping of the potter. But this misses the point of Jeremiah's message. In that lesson the clay (Israel) is resistant to the potter's goal so he has to change, not his ultimate intention, but the shape of the vessel he is using. Actually this object lesson anticipates the major reshaping that occurred with the realization of God's redemptive intention in Jesus. God's faithfulness was unfailing, Israel's faithlessness did not invalidate that (see Romans 3:1-4).

God's covenant with Abraham is finally fulfilled in its full redemptive significance in Jesus Christ. The consummation of the promise had awaited the time when Israel's faithfulness would qualify her to be the redemptive race but she had consistently remained part of the problem rather than the solution. Therefore, it came to pass that God kept his promise to Abraham through the life, death, and resurrection of "one faithful Israelite." This expression of God's faithfulness is why Paul can say in Romans 3:21-22, "But now, apart from law, the righteousness of God has been disclosed, and is attested by the law and the prophets, the righteousness of God through the faithfulness of Jesus Christ." We have become accustom to reading *righteousness* as having to do with uprightness, conformity to an ethical standard, or something like that. No one word in English can sum up the broad sense of the Hebrew and Greek words but for our purposes the meaning that relates most directly to our subject may be simply stated as *covenant faithfulness*. God's righteousness as covenant faithfulness is the theme that informs the entire book of Romans.

Paul emphasizes this point at the very outset of the Roman letter by referring to the "gospel of God, which he promised beforehand through his prophets in the Holy Scriptures," in which "the righteousness of God is revealed" (1:2, 16). God's indictment of Israel along with the Gentiles, he argues, does not "nullify the faithfulness of God" (3:3). The way God finally manifested his covenant faithfulness (righteousness) was a puzzle for many, certainly for Israel herself. In the prevailing Jewish perspective in the period known as Second Temple Judaism, the expectation of how God would fulfill his promises had very specific elements. In the first place it would bring an end to the exile. The Assyrians had already annihilated the northern kingdom of Israel. The hope that the nation of Judah would become the kingdom of God had been dashed in 587 B.C. by the Babylonians. All the pre-exilic prophets had predicted that catastrophic event. Moses had anticipated it in his farewell address (Deut. 30). In spite of the popular belief that Jerusalem and the Temple were inviolate because they were God's special province, disaster came to both.

Not only had prophets like Isaiah, Jeremiah and Ezekiel predicted the inevitability of the captivity because of Israel's faithlessness, they also had declared that, following a period of exile, God would restore the people in a "new exodus" that would usher in a period of universal peace. When the Medes and Persians overthrew Babylon and Cyrus the Persian became the reigning monarch, he gave permission to the Jews to return to their homeland. Those who chose to take advantage of this opportunity returned to a devastated country expecting to rebuild the Temple and experience the fulfillment of the prophetic vision of a golden age. The Temple was rebuilt, such as it was, but the restoration community was very different from what the exiles had anticipated.

The glory of God, the divine presence, did not return to the Temple, and they were still under the domination of pagan powers. This sense of continuing exile still prevailed at the time of Jesus. When would the humiliation finally end with the Romans being routed? When would the promised Messiah come and bring vindication and fulfillment?

Extensive research into Jewish literature of the years preceding and during the life of Jesus makes clear that nowhere in all this literature is the slightest suggestion that the great promises and prophecies of Isaiah, Jeremiah, Ezekiel and the rest—including those of Deuteronomy 30, which were important for Paul—had been fulfilled. Nevertheless, the hope remained that one day Israel would once again have the vision of the *glory* of her God in the Temple. Hope for the end of all exile, it was expected, would become actual with the appearance of an anointed one who would overthrow the pagan power (Rome) by revolutionary might and establish Israel once again as an independent nation in the world, as had been the case under David. The old Latin Christmas hymn captures this truth:

> O come, O come Immanuel,
> and Ransom Captive Israel;
> That mourns in lowly exile here,
> Until the Son of God appear.

That God would keep his covenant promise to Abraham as God did was beyond comprehension. God would address the Adam problem through a young Galilean prophet named Jesus. Instead of overthrowing Rome, he would be executed at their hands! His disciples could only conclude that Jesus was, like several other revolutionary leaders who had been executed, a failed messiah (cf. Luke 24). It took his resurrection to both vindicate Jesus and his message and the covenant faithfulness of God.

This dramatic outcome is what Saul of Tarsus came to see on the Damascus Road. His encounter with the risen Jesus resulted in nothing short of a worldview transformation. His proclamation that the crucified and risen Jesus was the Messiah of Israel, the one and only true Lord of the world, arose out of that encounter. Hence, the only appropriate response to this good news was to "confess with your mouth that Jesus is Lord and believe in your heart that God raised him from the dead" (Rom. 10:9). God's promise had been fulfilled!

Another unexpected outcome of God's covenant faithfulness was the response to this gospel of a crucified Messiah. Although the earliest followers of "the Way" were Jews, in the course of time the Gentiles became the most numerous believers. This development resulted in the new movement becoming largely a Gentile religion. If the covenant with Abraham was made with both him and his descendents, then it seemed that God's faithfulness had been thwarted. This anomaly explains why the burning issue in the early church concerned the question of the relation of Jew and Gentile. Does a Gentile have to become a Jew and accept the marks of Israel according to the flesh (notably circumcision) in order to be an authentic follower of the messiah Jesus? Paul was at the center of the controversy. He had come to see that this universal response to the gospel was the intention of God's covenant with Abraham from the beginning.

These unexpected developments lay behind the often-controversial chapters nine, ten, and eleven of Romans. What Paul is doing is demonstrating the covenant faithfulness of God to Israel by redefining *Israel*, consistent with the promise to Abraham to create one worldwide family composed of both Jew and Gentile. The redefined *Israel* is now identified, not by the marks of "flesh" but by faith in Jesus as God's Messiah.

So it is that the faithfulness of God has been fully vindicated through the person and work of Messiah Jesus. He had manifested the faithfulness to which the descendents of Abraham were called, but who had become part of the problem rather than the agents of its solution. What does it mean to be God's holy people today? The meaning begins by climbing Mount Moriah and realizing from that vantage point what God has promised and that he is always faithful to that promise. It means embracing the promise fulfilled in Jesus and coming by faith to live out in the present the yet-coming fullness of the kingdom of God.

As we look to the future, our faith is based on the faithfulness of the Lord that was demonstrated in keeping his promises to Abraham. We experience now the life of the "age to come" by identification through faith and baptism with Christ and live in the full assurance that God will, in his own time and wisdom bring an end to all evil and fully establish the kingdom of God at the consummation of history

Reflections

In the rough and tumble of daily living, it is important for spiritual and mental health to have a certain level of stability. Our relationships depend on it. Our business transactions depend on it. Society depends on it. Even the possibility of meaningful communication depends on it. What is true in every other area of life is equally true in our religious life. The possibility of a flourishing spiritual life depends on the nature of the God who is the object of worship. Pagan deities were unpredictable because their desires and requirements were reflections of the priests who supposedly mediated their requirements to their followers.

The uniqueness of the God of Abraham, Isaac, and Jacob is his character of dependableness. Unlike pagan deities, he gave his word in a covenant relation and his followers could "take it to the bank." Throughout the Old Testament, the Israelite prophets and poets celebrated this character of Yahweh, even when the specific word is not present. It is encountered on the threshold of human history following the great flood that only Noah and his family survived. God gave his word to never again destroy his creation by water and gave the rainbow as the symbol of his faithfulness to that word (Gen. 9:12-15). One could say that the most enduring concept of Yahweh's nature throughout the Old Testament is his faithfulness in keeping his word.

The focus of this chapter is on God's commitment to Abraham and his descendents. However, the significance of this commitment is missed if it is understood as the election of a people to be the exclusive recipients of God's favor and blessing. That was, as history has clearly demonstrated, the way in which the popular concept of Israel's election was perverted. The true significance is found in God's intention for Israel to be the instrument through which he will redeem his creation.

Like our own lives, the ups and downs of Israel's history meant that there were times when it was difficult to have faith that God was keeping his word. One of the most difficult of those times for the faithful in Israel was the destruction of the nation, its capital of Jerusalem and the Temple in 587 B.C. This event was a crushing blow to Israel's faith because it really did seem that the Lord had been unable to protect his people. We sense the despair of the captives in the lament of Psalm 137: "By the rivers of Babylon—there we sat down and there we wept when we remembered Zion. On the willows there, we hung up our harps. For there our captors asked us for songs, and our tormentors asked for mirth, saying, 'Sing us one of the songs of Zion!' How could we sing the Lord's song in a foreign land?" Many children of God can identify with this sense of alienation and defeat and have "hung their harps on the (weeping) willows."

However, there is more! The compiler of the Psalter demonstrates the tenacity of Israel's faith by sandwiching this profound lament between two psalms that celebrate God's faithfulness. In Psalm 136, with monotonous repetition in each of the 26 verses, the psalmist gives thanks based on God's acts of deliverance in the Exodus and his oversight of nature. All manifested his "steadfast love." This meaning is the rendering of *chesed* that, as noted earlier, is the Hebrew word that encapsulates the covenant faithfulness of the Lord. Psalm 138 likewise celebrates God's faithfulness, beautifully summarized in vvs. 7-8: "Though I walk in the midst of trouble you preserve me against the wrath of my enemies; you stretch out your hand, and your right hand delivers me. The Lord will fulfill his purpose for me; your *steadfast love*, O Lord, endures forever."

So devastating was the Babylonian conquest that one entire book of the Old Testament was dedicated to a sustained lament over it. But at the heart of the writer's description of the total destruction that should have put an end to all hope, the writer pulls himself up to full stature, looks to the future beyond the heartbreak and judgment, and declares, "But this I call to mind, and therefore I have hope: The *steadfast love* of the Lord never ceases, his mercies never come to an end; they are new every morning; great is your faithfulness" (Lam. 3:21-24).

Many of God's people through the ages have found themselves in situations that tested their faith to the breaking point. It took great courage to persevere in those trying times. One of the lessons learned from the biblical narrative is the fact that God's faithfulness does not always manifest itself in the way we expect. His promise to address the problem of Adam took a radically different direction than the popular hope had envisioned. W. T. Purkiser used to tell a story about a man who sought to encourage his son to get a college education by promising him that if he would do so, upon graduation he would buy him a horse and buggy. During the son's years of college, the automobile was invented and the father bought his son a car. He really kept his word, but in an unexpected fashion.

Ultimately, the cross and resurrection of Jesus stand as an enacted promise and thus as a beacon of hope that God's promises will not fail. That fact is why Paul could encourage his churches by appealing to the faithfulness of God: "He will also strengthen you to the end, so that you may be blameless on the day of our Lord Jesus Christ. God is faithful; by him you were called into the fellowship of his Son, Jesus Christ our Lord" (1 Cor. 1:8-9).

The death and resurrection of Christ inaugurated a new order of being referred to in the New Testament variously as "the age to come" or the "new creation." The emphasis is on the idea of "inauguration." The prophetic hope of the Old Covenant was that God would finally put an end to evil, but clearly, that end did not occur. In Jesus, the kingdom of God had become a present reality and Satan and the powers had been defeated, but they were still active in the world. Has God's faithfulness failed?

Standing in the ruins of the Third Reich lecturing on the Apostles' Creed, Karl Barth put this matter in perspective using the imagery of a chess game:

> The game is won, even though the player can still play a few further moves. Actually, he is almost mated. The clock has run down, even though the pendulum still swings a few times this way and that. It is in this interim space that we are living: the old is past, behold it has all become new. The Easter message tells us that our enemies, sin, the curse and death, are beaten. Ultimately they can no longer start mischief. They still behave as though the game was not decided, the battle not fought; we must still reckon with them, but fundamentally we must cease to fear them anymore. If you have heard the Easter message, you can no longer run around with a

tragic face and lead the humorless existence of a man who has no hope. One thing still holds, and this one thing is really serious, that Jesus is the Victory.[12]

Is this optimistic word whistling in the dark? Two thousand years have transpired, and the consummation of this victory has not appeared. There have been many fits and starts, unfulfilled predictions, and probably much skepticism. St. Peter faced the same situation in his day but insisted on reliance on the faithfulness of God to ultimately keep his word: "First of all you must understand this, that in the last days scoffers will come, scoffing and indulging their own lusts and saying, 'Where is the promise of his coming? For ever since our ancestors died all things are as they were from the beginning of creation!'. . . But do not ignore this one fact, beloved, that with the Lord one day is like a thousand years, and a thousand years are like one day. The Lord is not slow about his promise, as some think of slowness, but is patient with you, not wanting any to perish, but all to come to repentance" (2 Pet. 3:3-9).

If we are to understand and experience the faithfulness of God in our own lives, we must understand the biblical concept of faith. Faith has a variety of meanings in scripture but the meaning that is relevant to this issue is "trust." Trust is more than and different from "wishful thinking." It is, of necessity, a relation to a promise, whether expressed or implied. This relation simply means that God's faithfulness pertains to his keeping a promise. The implication is that only when a promise has been made can there be faith. Annie Johnson Flint perceptively captures the difference between faith and wishful hoping:

> God hath not promised skies always blue,
> Flower-strewn pathways all our lives thro';
> God hath not promised sun without rain,
> Joy without sorrow, peace without pain.
>
> 'But God hath promised strength for the day,
> Rest for the labor, light for the way,
> Grace for the trials, help from above,
> Unfailing sympathy, undying love.

---

[12]Karl Barth, *Dogmatics in Outline* (London: SCM Press, 1960), 123.

Many people appear to think that they can exercise faith for whatever they want and God will honor it. But the fact is that if God has not made a promise, we cannot have faith. This statement is but another way of saying that we cannot have faith for anything that is not in accord with God's will. This seems to be the significance of James 5:15. There is a direct statement that if one has sinned, she *will be* forgiven. However the healing of sickness is dependant on the "prayer of faith." It is thus proper for one to "seek to offer the prayer of faith." It is not the consequence of desire or a self-generated assertion of will but a trust in God's revealed will. In a word, authentic faith always prays "according to your will." I once heard a famous "healing televangelist" say that we should never pray this because it weakens faith. Unfortunately, this is the stuff out of which presumption is made. And presumption got Pharaoh's army drowned (Heb. 11:29).

How do we know God's will? How can we identify a divine promise? The most certain way is from the word of God. However, not every "promise" in scripture can automatically, or arbitrarily, be taken as a promise "to me." One way of describing the authority of scripture is expressed by the formula, "the Bible has the power to become the Word of God." While that by itself is not an adequate explanation of biblical authority, it does convey how a text may become God's word to us. There are times when a scriptural word leaps off the page with existential power and we are overwhelmed with the realization that God is actually addressing us personally. When the God of Abraham, Isaac and Jacob has truly given us his word, and our faith has responded, its reality becomes "the substance of things hoped for and the evidence of things not [yet] seen."

Questions to Think About

1. Have you had experiences in which you believed God had made a promise to you?
2. Were you able to validate the promise by biblical teaching?
3. Have you been tempted at times to believe that God's delay was denial?
4. Has God ever kept his word to you in a totally unexpected fashion?

Chapter Three

MOUNT SINAI

Revelation of the Holiness of God

The Lord said to Moses: "Go to the people and consecrate them today and tomorrow. Have them wash their clothes and prepare for the third day, because on the third day the Lord will come down upon Mount Sinai in the sight of all the people. You shall set limits for the people all around, saying, 'Be careful not to go up the mountain or to touch the edge of it. Any who touch the mountain shall be put to death.... When the trumpet sounds a long blast, they may go up on the mountain'." So Moses went down from the mountain to the people. He consecrated the people, and they washed their clothes. And he said to the people, "Prepare for the third day".... (Ex. 19:10-15).

Mount Sinai

The traditional location of Mount Sinai/Horeb is near the southern tip of the Sinai Peninsula. Since there is some difficulty with this location, scholars have offered other proposed sites. But none of them can be made to fit all the Old Testament data. Hence, the precise geographical site is uncertain. Nonetheless, the meaning of the events that transpired on or near this mountain is abundantly clear and definitive for the entire biblical story as a revelation of the nature of God and his relation to his people as well as the holy life to which they are called.

While the events at Sinai embody a number of important theological truths, the revelation of the *holiness* of God stands out as a significant advance in Israel's understanding of her God, whose name they have come to know as Yahweh (cf. Ex. 6:3). It was on this same ground that Moses had encountered the divine holiness in the burning bush incident. That incident contained the first explicit reference to holiness in Scripture (Ex. 3:5). Now the people themselves must become aware of this aspect of the God who had rescued them from Egyptian slavery. They had learned that it was God's faithfulness in keeping his promises to Abraham, Isaac and Jacob that had been the divine reason for that mighty act of deliverance. They had learned that he was "Jehoveh-Jireh" in providing food and water in the desert. But their knowledge of his essential nature of holiness awaited the encounter at the "mountain of God."

As suggested, this lesson was anticipated by Moses' experience of God's presence at the burning bush. When the shepherd approached the strange sight, the voice from within it told him to take off his sandals because it was holy ground. What made it holy? It was the presence of the Lord since, as will become clear, only that which is or has been in relation to Him can be holy. No place is holy within itself, only in relation to the Holy One. The instruction to Moses to remove his sandals furthermore makes it clear that nothing can approach that which is holy without a preparation that removes whatever is impure or profane. Briefly stated, *purity is the requirement for coming into contact with the holy God.*

The events at Sinai not only taught the people *that* Yahweh was holy, but also the *meaning and significance* of his holiness for the divine-human relation. They came to see that holiness refers to God's innermost essence, his quintessential being, his deity in contrast to all things creaturely.[13] This means that God is "wholly Other." In this sense holiness communicates God's transcendence. Yet God as holy is neither remote nor unknowable. The wholly Other is also wholly present.

One of the most important implications of this understanding of the holiness of God is that his holiness is not primarily a moral attribute, as if it meant merely the perfect goodness of some super being with a white beard. Rather it refers to that absolute "otherness" that distinguishes the divine from all that is creaturely, and so characterizes every aspect of God. Every attribute of God must be prefaced by this qualification. For

---

[13]The Hebrew would not have expressed this truth in this philosophical way but in more practical ways.

instance, this is why we must refer to God as "holy love." We shall explore the significance of this meaning below.

Inherent and Derived Holiness

The fundamental implication of a proper understanding of holiness is that only God is *inherently holy*. Places, persons, objects, or times are holy only as the result of their relation to God. This is where the definition of "sanctification" as "setting apart" is relevant. Holiness is applied to whatever and whoever is sanctified, i.e. set apart, or devoted to Deity. In things and in people, holiness is always derivative. It expresses a relationship with God. Dennis Kinlaw states it succinctly, "The OT may differentiate between things that are clean and unclean, but it knows nothing that is holy apart from its relation to God."[14] This implies that the derived holiness of ordinary realities is a *status*, and does not involve any inherent quality that has been communicated or possessed. The holiness of the mountain, for instance, is not an inherent holiness but is relational in nature and therefore derived from the fact that God "dwells" there.

The truth of this observation is vividly illustrated in reverse by the incident reported in 1 Samuel 4:1-10. The people mistakenly assumed that the Ark of the Covenant had an inherent quality independent of its proper relation to God and could serve as a battle symbol that would automatically give them victory over the Philistines. This belief was obviously a faulty assumption with devastating consequences.

This understanding means that Israel could be called a holy nation (Ex. 19:6) by virtue of *derived* holiness, a status consequent upon being sanctified, i.e. set apart for a special relation to God. Scripture describes this status of being a "holy people" in various ways (Ex. 19:5-6; Titus 2:14; 1 Pet. 2:9-10), all referring to a unique relationship. This status was given by God to those who had been qualified by rituals of purification, i.e., sanctified. The incompatibility of the holy with the unclean is the basis of the need for a preparatory cleansing or purification. As Gordon Wenham explains, "Everything that is not holy is common. Common things divide into two groups, the clean and the unclean. Clean things become holy, when they are sanctified. But unclean objects cannot be sanctified. Clean things can be made unclean, if they are polluted. Finally, holy items may be defiled and become

---

[14]Dennis Kinlaw, "Old Testament Roots of the Wesleyan Message," *Further Insights Into Holiness* (K.C.: Beacon Hill Press, 1963), 44

common, even polluted, and therefore unclean."[15] This fact explains the preparation required of the people prior to God's descent on the mountain. Their preparation involved cleansing themselves from any defilement by that which was profane. "Profane," does not mean "unholy" but any thing that had not been ritually purified. *Only that which had been cleansed could be sanctified or consecrated to God.*

The clothes that had been worn in normal life must be "washed," not primarily to remove the physical dirt but to remove any ritual impurity. Couples were not to engage in sexual intercourse, which resulted in a temporary state of impurity. These preparations illustrate the truth that "holiness" refers to that which is unapproachable except through divinely imposed restrictions or that which is withdrawn from common use.

Ethical Holiness

It is at this point that we can engage the question of the moral or ethical implications of the holiness of God for the life of those who are God's "holy people." We have seen that they are holy in terms of *status based on their relation to God.* It is this status that is the basis for the requirement of ethical holiness. It involves a call to live out their status as a holy people, which involves a lifestyle that is determined by the holiness of God rightly understood. Who God is, the holy one, is determinative of the ethical manifestation of the special relation of his people to him. It is important to recognize that this lifestyle is *response* and not participation. For Israel, this response is spelled out in the ten words constituting the Decalogue and involves two relations: to God and to other things and persons.

Since God is holy in the sense emphasized here, the logical implication is that he is alone qualified for an exclusive place in the life of his people. Joshua makes this point explicitly in the final convocation prior to the dispersing of the tribes to their inheritance in the Promised Land (Joshua 24:19-20). Oddly enough, the Hebrews were still holding on to the gods of their ancestors. They responded to Joshua's call for commitment by professing to add the worship of Yahweh to these ancestral deities. But, recognizing their intention, Joshua declared that

---

[15] Gordon J. Wenham, *The Book of Leviticus* (Grand Rapids: William B. Eerdmans Pub. Co., 1979), 29.

they could not do this because Yahweh "is a holy god, a jealous god." God has no peers and will tolerate no rivals.

This also is the clear implication of the first three words of the Decalogue: no other gods before me; no images of me (idolatry); no misuse of my holy name. The seventh day (a time) has been sanctified (set apart) and therefore has the status of holy and is thus to be reverenced. All persons incorporated in the covenant community, including their property, are holy because of their *status* of being related to God. Persons are to be respected and treated as nothing less than persons created in God's image. Thus, *the ethical aspect of holiness is derivative of God's holiness rather than an inherent participation in his nature.* This fact is why the repeated call for holiness says, "Be holy *because* God is holy," not *as* he is holy.

A proper understanding of the nature of this call for ethical holiness ("*because* God is holy") is extremely important for an appropriate perception of the character of the holy life. Unfortunately, it has often been interpreted as if the call was to be holy *as* God is holy thus implying that the holiness of God can be communicated to his people. This has been one of the issues that have plagued the "holiness movement" from its earliest days. This problem partly resulted from misinterpreting God's holiness as moral in nature. This interpretation appears to make it possible to see a correlation between God's holiness and that of his people. This conclusion was drawn by most teachers of the nineteenth-century holiness movement. One prominent spokesman declared: "In a sense holiness in man is the same as holiness in God for there are not two kinds of holiness." But a much more biblical understanding of holiness would say that Israel could not achieve or even imitate Yahweh's holiness. There is an unbridgeable gap between them. In summary, *a pattern for properly understanding the relation between the Holy One and his holy people is clearly demonstrated theologically by the revelation of the holiness of God at Mt. Sinai.* This pattern helps in recognizing multiple meanings of "sanctification," which has been confusing to many. The term "sanctification" may refer to the act of separation to a holy God, a relation that results in a status of "holy" or "sanctified." Once this status has been granted, the term can then refer to the consecration of what (or who) has been cleansed or purified to the worship and service of God. Therefore, it is biblically and theologically appropriate to refer to those who have been qualified for the status of holiness by purification and consequently related to God as the "sanctified," (cf. 1 Cor. 1:2). The consecration of those who have been qualified in this way to "be sanctified" has for its intention the ethical aspect of holiness.

St. Paul is probably referring to this ethical stage of the Christian life in identifying believers as "called to be saints," or "holy ones" (Rom. 1:7; 1 Cor. 1:2). This is the theological understanding that informs his appeal in Romans: "Do you not know that if you present yourselves to anyone as obedient slaves, you are slaves of the one whom you obey, either of sin, which leads to death, or of obedience, which leads to righteousness? But thanks be to God that you, having once been slaves of sin, have become obedient from the heart to the form of teaching to which you were entrusted, and that you, having been set free from sin, have become slaves of righteousness.... For just as you once presented your members as slaves to impurity and to greater and greater iniquity, so now present your members as slaves to righteousness for sanctification" (Rom. 6:17-22). Here we have both aspects of "sanctification" expressed in terms of their function as we have analyzed them. The believers have become holy in status and consequently are now in a position to consecrate themselves to the pursuit of the ideal of ethical holiness.

Holiness and Worship

The experience of the holiness of God at Mount Sinai has implications for worship. Even though the proper rituals of purification had been performed this did not qualify them for intimacy with the Divine since the mountain was holy, not in itself, but because it had been in relation to God. Hence it was dangerous, even deadly, for people or animals to infringe on this holiness (19:12). When the formal worship setting and rituals were later put in place, this same careful preparation was necessary for those who served in the sanctuary. The one chosen to make the annual entry into the holy of holies had to make *special* preparation. It was also true that there had to be holiness in the camp as well as in the tabernacle.

New Testament worship does not abandon the holiness of God in favor of a shallow intimacy. While it is true that love is the primary emphasis of the divine nature as revealed in the New Testament, it must be understood as "holy love" and not shallow sentimentality. The worship that goes on in "heaven" while worship is occurring in the space-time realm is characterized by the celebration of God's holiness as the angels recite "Holy, holy, holy. The Lord God the Almighty, who was and is and is to come" (Rev. 3:8). In like manner, authentic worship is not a pep rally or theatre presentation but a celebration of who God is in both being and action. It should be marked by an aura of reverence in the presence of "the Holy One of Israel."

The Call to Holy Living

Furthermore, the full implication of the events surrounding Sinai can be helpful to many who have struggled with the belief that God has called them to a level of holy living that they have never been able to realize. As I have traveled across the country preaching and teaching in holiness churches, I have concluded that there are more former adherents to these communions than present ones. How does one explain this disturbing phenomenon?

I am convinced that many, having sought the level of "perfection" to which they had been called and finding it unattainable became discouraged and retired from the battle. They settled for a context that did not call for such an experience. I am also convinced that this did not need to happen, and would not have happened if the biblical truth of holiness had been more soundly preached.

Entire sanctification has often been emphasized as a "second work of grace," and the exegesis of the Sinai encounter demonstrates that theologically this is appropriate. The experience of Israel at the holy mountain clearly reflects two stages of experience. They were first cleansed as preparation for coming into relation to God and subsequently consecrated themselves to observe the conditions of the covenant. The question is what is the nature of this second work[16] of grace? The fact that it was "second" does not within itself give an adequate answer to the question since "experience" is ambiguous. The content and nature of experience may take various forms, including merely emotional. If biblical revelation is to be taken seriously, all experience can be evaluated in the light of the Mount Sinai revelation. Thus, the biblical understanding of the holiness of God and God's call for his people to "be holy *because* he is holy" is essential for understanding the nature of this "second work of grace." How did the present situation in the holiness movement develop?

---

[16]The term "work" can be quite misleading as it might suggest a unilateral action on God's part but certainly not something performed by unaided human endeavor. I simply adopt the popular term in order to show the possibility of the relation of good exegesis to folk theology.

The Theology of Wesley's Successors

In the nineteenth century, especially during the post-Civil War period, there was a widespread spiritual awakening characterized by many Christians professing to have received a "deeper spiritual experience" which many came to call "entire sanctification." This movement grew out of the revival in England in the eighteenth century associated with the names of John and Charles Wesley. The developments in the nineteenth century took on a somewhat different flavor from that preached by the Wesleys and resulted in the formation of several "holiness" denominations determined to preserve the results of that movement of the Spirit.

One of the most influential factors that shaped the prevailing theological understanding of the period came from the general culture of the late nineteenth century. It was an age of optimism. There was a general belief in the perfectibility of the human race. This ethos made it seem feasible to make "extravagant claims" for the experience of entire sanctification.

Another influencing factor was the shift of emphasis from the Wesleys--who were primarily concerned with the *content* of sanctification--to a primary stress in the American holiness movement of the next century on the *structure* of the experience. The result was that holiness teachers and preachers tended to scour the Bible for any evidence of "two works of grace," giving little attention to generally accepted principles of proper biblical interpretation. John Wesley had developed his understanding of sanctification in dialog with the classical theological development of the Christian church. By some contrast, the popular teaching of the later holiness movement became a one-issue theology. In fact, they generally cut themselves off from the developments in the larger world of theology, philosophy, and psychology.

The holy life came to be identified with "puritan" standards of behavior. Many of the preachers of the holiness movement equated holiness with the avoidance of secret societies, all worldly amusements, wearing of gold, pearls, and costly or gaudy apparel, and the use of opium, morphine, and tobacco. One report identified holiness preaching with the denunciation of "the wearing of gold and feathers and flowers," and the "filthiness of tobacco and snuff." As L.W. Munhall said in defending the traditional standards of conduct of the Methodist church:

"Holiness unto the Lord, and separation from the fashions, fads and frivolities of the world were, in the minds and consciences of the earlier Methodists, inseparable. Mr. Wesley's Rule, which forbade, 'taking such diversions as cannot be used in the name of the Lord Jesus,' and which became a disciplinary rule, was, by all good Methodists, believed to forbid dancing, card-playing, and theatre going."[17]

At a more theological level, there was a significant shift of emphasis from Mr. Wesley. This shift pertains to the goal or *telos* of sanctification, for without a goal it is impossible to have an understanding of the process of spiritual growth. This issue turns out to be a pivotal watershed. The nineteenth-century holiness movement generally interpreted the goal of sanctification to be freedom from sin, a negative concept. The difficulties were intensified by some early preachers who, based on this "goal," preached "holiness or hell." By contrast, earlier Wesleyan theology saw the goal of sanctification to be the renewal of humanity in the image of God. The difference is subtle but significant.

With the collapse of the nineteenth-century spirit of optimism under the impact of two world wars, the great depression, and the accompanying developments in depth psychology that called attention to the pervasiveness of sin in human nature, the high expectations for the results of "entire sanctification" began to weaken. Throughout the 20th century the optimism about what would occur in an experience of entire sanctification began to be more and more tempered as the early claims became less and less credible. The claims were modified and more and more place was given to human infirmities resulting from the fallen nature of humanity.

The widespread experience of confusion and disillusionment arising from interpreting the human experience of sanctification or holiness in terms of "freedom from sin" has been very hurtful in church life. Such interpretation fails to recognize the simple fact that the call to holiness in 1 Peter 1:14-16 is not a call to be holy *as* God is holy, but *because* he is holy. As one person testified, "I find all this quite intolerable. It is not that it were somehow irrational for God to call me to be holy (Heb. 12:14). The command itself makes sense, but I have a problem of another kind. I am unholy, and try as I may I cannot convince myself that I shall ever measure up to this standard—the holiness of God." This has been the experience of many Christians. In

---

[17]L.W.Munhall, *Breakers! Methodism Adrift* (N.Y.: Charles C. Cook, 1913), 166.

response to this, the understanding of the holiness of God as explored in the first part of this chapter opens the door to a picture of the holy life that is true to both Scripture and actual human experience. As John Wesley emphasized, the validity of any doctrine about experience must be tested in the actual lives of believers. It is here that the theological rubber meets the road. Therefore, let me suggest what I have found to be a biblically sound and an experientially compelling understanding of an experience that takes seriously the call to holiness.

Reflections

From early in the post-Civil War holiness movement, entire sanctification was interpreted as a work of grace that "purified the heart" from inbred or original sin. However, based on the biblical understanding, as was demonstrated by the exegesis above, purity is the *prerequisite* for sanctification rather than its result. It is crucial to see that this purity is a ritualistic concept rather than the removal of a foreign "substance" from the soul, which is the way it was popularly explained. This prerequisite is the reason holiness is best interpreted initially as a *status*. In this sense, every person (or group) who enters into a saving relation to God is thereby *holy*. This relationship is established in what might be termed a "first work of grace." This status involves a cleansing resulting from pardon or the forgiveness of sins that produces purity as the necessary prerequisite to "sanctification." This dual meaning creates an apparent ambiguity since the New Testament uses the concept of "sanctification" (*hagiazō*) to refer both to the initial relationship (1 Cor. 1:2) and the further event of "consecration" based on that relationship (Romans 12:1-2).

This initial cleansing is captured in the once popular invitation hymn by Elisha A. Huffman (1878) that refers to conversion and not to a "second blessing."

> Have you been to Jesus for the cleansing power?
> Are you washed in the blood of the Lamb?
> Are you fully trusting in His grace this hour?
> Are you washed in the blood of the Lamb?
>
> Lay aside the garments that are stained with sin
> Are you washed in the blood of the Lamb?
> There's a fountain flowing for the soul unclean?

O be washed in blood of the Lamb!

Having been "cleansed by the blood of the Lamb," the believer is now in a position to consecrated herself to the pursuit of the ethical aspect of holiness, which is centrally understood in the New Testament as embodied in the concept of the image of God (cf. Rom. 8:29; 2 Cor. 3:18).This act of consecration, theologically (not necessarily chronologically) subsequent to the event of cleansing, is a viable way of interpreting the experience of "entire sanctification." It is the whole-hearted, whole person presentation of a cleansed person to the service and worship of God that involves not full attainment but active and intentional pursuit of the ideal of Christlikeness. This spiritual pursuit of restoration of the image of God does not presuppose a rigid, pre-determined structure of experience or a required level of conformity. Too many factors enter into the picture to create a single pattern of spiritual experience into which all persons should be directed. Experience is dynamic and must be allowed freedom under the sovereignty of God and the work of the Holy Spirit.

The "educational process" implicit in this study of the holiness of God reminds us of the importance of constantly pursuing a more perfect comprehension of biblical truth. Virtually no one begins the Christian life with a full-blown grasp of all the implications of their conversion. Like Abraham, Moses and the people of Israel, learning to know who God is and the implications of this knowledge for daily living is an ongoing enterprise. This fact is doubtless the basis for the exhortation in Hebrews 6:1 to "leave behind the basic teaching about Christ" and go on toward perfection (maturity).

The history of the American Holiness revivals of the 19th century demonstrates the importance of this process of growth in understanding. Early and elementary perceptions, if inadequate, can lead to unfortunate practical problems. The fact that these revivals operated on a non-biblical interpretation of God's holiness clearly demonstrates this result. They eventually came to an identity crisis, even being pronounced dead by several of their leaders, because of this misunderstanding and its implications. Further, with the development of biblical scholars within the movement committed to biblical integrity, the recognition of a proper view of God's holiness as reflected in the Sinai revelation has pointed the way out of the impasse.

Rightly understood, the pursuit of the holy life is not a burdensome attempt to replicate the holiness of God. It is a joyful, fulfilling and meaningful pilgrimage toward a goal that makes one more and more the human being God intended. The clue to this lifelong experience is the biblical understanding of the relation between holiness as a *status* and holiness as an ethical lifestyle revealed in the Sinai encounter. It helps us understand the diverse uses of the term *sanctify* in the New Testament. But apart from its significance for biblical interpretation, it clarifies the basis of the holy life.

The failure of much of the teaching of the early modern holiness movement to recognize this truth resulted in "extravagant claims" for an experience they called "entire sanctification." These claims, in turn, ultimately resulted in a "credibility gap" with a generation that more and more discovered the "intractable nature of sin." More than one of my peers has related to me their frustration over the inability of the early message they heard to make good on its claims for experience. One close friend shared how her mother, the wife of a denominational leader, was a repeated seeker at a public altar because she could never experience what was preached. Finally, she told me, her father instructed his wife to desist since these repeated visits to the altar looked bad for his reputation. Her mother lived out her life in frustration.

This relation also provides us with a viable and biblically grounded concept of what might be called, based on 1 Thessalonians 5:23-4, "entire sanctification." Contrary to a popular (mis)interpretation by early holiness teaching, it does not refer to "a complete [and final] cleansing from all sin." That would be participating in the holiness of God. Rather, entire sanctification can be defined as the "whole hearted, whole person commitment to the pursuit of the image of God characterized by love to God and others."

Having been "cleansed" and made ceremonially pure by the forgiveness of sins and brought into a relation to God by grace, i.e. initially sanctified, we are qualified to present ourselves a "living sacrifice" to God.

Questions to Think About

1. How does the "holiness preaching" you have heard relate to the analysis of this chapter?
2. How does this understanding of holiness offer a viable relationship between a "crisis"
   and a "process" in spiritual experience?

3. Do you think the holiness model of experience as described in this chapter could contribute to the revitalization of today's "holiness movement?"
4. Does holiness as described in this chapter address personal issues you have confronted in your Christian life?

Chapter 4

Mounts Ebal and Gerizim

Revelation of Covenant Renewal

"So when you have crossed over the Jordan, you shall set up these stones, about which I am commanding you today, on Mount Ebal; and you shall cover them with plaster. And you shall build an altar there to the Lord your God, an altar of stones on which you have not used an iron tool. You must build the altar of the Lord your God of unhewn stones. Then offer up burnt offerings on it to the Lord your God, make sacrifices of well-being, and eat them there, rejoicing before the Lord your God. You shall write on the stones all the words of this law very clearly. . . The same day Moses charged the people as follows: When you have crossed over the Jordan, these shall stand on Mount Gerizim for the blessing of the people: . . . And these shall stand on Mount Ebal for the curse." Deuteronomy 27:4-8; 11-12a; 13a.

Photo of Mt. Gerizim by H. Ray Dunning

While touring the land of Israel, near Jacob's well (according to our guide the only certain geographical location of any event in Jesus' life) we came across a site where two mounds appeared to be facing each other with a valley between them where the town of Nablus is now located. When we were facing east the one on our right was covered with verdant green vegetation. The one on the left was very bare, with no vegetation in sight. These hills were Mount Gerizim and Mount Ebal, providing a perfect visual representation of the instructions of Moses to the people in Deuteronomy 11:29—"When the Lord your God has brought you into the land that you are entering to occupy, you shall set the blessing on Mount Gerizim and the curse on Mount Ebal."

This location was the site where the Israelites were to renew the covenant with Yahweh after crossing the Jordan and beginning to occupy the land (Deut. 27:1-9). These two mountains are located near the site of Shechem, which had very early associations with Israel's religious history. Shechem is named in Genesis 12:6-8 as the place where Abraham reached the "great tree of Moreh" and offered sacrifices. This event would remind them of the promise of the land. Nearby was the tomb of Joseph (Joshua 24:32) that would recall their preservation from famine.

Deuteronomy 27:2-8 describes the preparation for the renewal ceremony, all of which had important theological implications. There were two parts to the preparation: first, they were to set up stones and plaster them with "whitewash." The "whole law" was to be written on them. Second, they were to build an altar upon which sacrifices were to be offered. We are not told what was to be written on the stones but in all likelihood, it was the 10 commandments as the basic expression of the law since the remainder of the covenant legislation was really a spelling out of specific implications of those principles. The purpose of these stones was no doubt to remind the Israelites every time they passed through this valley of the choices that faced them day by day and the serious consequences of those choices. As long as they honored the covenant requirements, they would be preserved in the land.

Of interest is the final emphasis on writing the law "clearly." One is reminded of the instructions to Habakkuk the prophet to "Write the vision; make it plain on tablets, so that a runner may read it" (Habakkuk 2:2). God wants the disclosure of himself and his intention for humanity to be understood without confusion. Not only must the inscription be legible but it must be such that the people can know what they are and how they are to respond to them. Martin Luther's advice to preachers is surely appropriate here: "So preach that when people depart they will be able to say, 'the preacher said *this*'." One of the most important responses any minister could receive from his or her parishioners is "I understood everything you were telling me."

The instructions for building the altar were intended to emphasize the holiness of God. The holiness of the altar is implicitly stressed in that the stones that were to compose it were not to be cut with iron instruments. Tools that had been used for secular or profane purposes would defile the stones by contact and this result was unacceptable. It is also possible that this stipulation reflected the fact that the Israelites had not at this time acquired the skill of iron working and tools of iron were only available from the Canaanites (1 Samuel 13:19f.). Thus, to use these Canaanite products might suggest a compromise with idolatry.

The sacrifices to be offered had great significance. The sacrifices offered at the original covenant ceremony were the burnt offering and the peace offering (Exodus 24:5). There were to be replicated at this ceremony. Taken together they represent both the people's relation to God and their relation to each other. Thus love for God and love for neighbor are present in the worship that celebrates the renewal of the covenant in the land. So even the Hebrew sacrificial system was designed from the beginning to teach the Israelites the inseparable nature of love for God and others.

As we have noted elsewhere in this study, these two relations are aspects of what it means for human persons to be created in the image of God. The third relation (to the land) is implicit in the narrative since this covenant renewal is to take place on the soil that God had promised Abraham and his descendents. Much of the legislation in Deuteronomy has reference to the land as the gift of God and therefore the ways in which Israel is to manifest stewardship of it. This emphasis is clearly based on the original creation at which God gave to Adam and Eve the charge of responsible stewardship over the non-human world.

This three-fold relation provides the framework for the theology and ethics of the Old Testament. It may be visualized in the form of an equilateral triangle. The apex of the triangle, the theological angle, is the relation to God; the other angles, the social and economic angles, refer to the other two: God, Israel and the land, in a triangle of relationships, each of which affected the others. The integrated relation between these three elements is why, as Moses predicts would eventually happen (Deut. 29:19—30:1), to be carried out of the land into exile was a complete calamity.

The renewal ritual itself had great symbolic significance. The twelve tribes were divided into two groups and positioned on the slopes of the hills facing each other like two choirs preparing to present an antiphonal response chorus. The priests stood in the middle of this natural amphitheatre with the Ark of the Covenant. Although it would have involved a meaningful action, it cannot be assumed that the groups on the two mountains spoke (or sang) at all. Their action in standing there may have simply been representative. There is probably also significance in Mount Gerizim—the luxuriant one—being on the right when facing east. Aged Israel blessing the two sons of Joseph in Genesis 48:8ff. suggests that the right hand was a sign of special blessing. The contrasting fertility and barrenness of the two mountains demonstrated the contrast between the two options facing the people. Obedience to the covenant requirements would result in blessing, disobedience would bring the curse upon them. Prior to the dispersion of the tribes to their respective locations in the land, Joshua gathered them at this same spot for another convocation or covenant renewal (Joshua 8:33-35) and called them to the same exclusive commitment to the Lord.

The focus of the passage on curses and blessings may suggest a kind of legalism but this conclusion would be to fail to understand the nature of the covenant that is being renewed by this ritual. We refer to this event as a covenant renewal because the definitive covenant that established the relation between Yahweh and Israel was consummated at Mount Sinai. The nature and terms of that covenant informed the renewal at Ebal/Gerizim.

Nature of the Covenant

Archeologists have discovered many examples of covenants in the Near East from the time of the Exodus. There were two types of these covenants. The first was an agreement between equals and is referred to as a *parity* covenant. Each partner had equal status so that the result was a negotiated relationship to which each party had input. It seems that the parties to this type of agreement referred to each other as "brothers." The second type was between unequals, usually between a Lord and his vassal or a dominant nation and a subordinate one that receives protection from the other and in response pays tribute and loyalty. This form of covenant is termed a *suzerainty* or *vassal* treaty. This latter type of covenant appears to provide the structural pattern for the Sinai Covenant.

The *suzerainty* covenant normally had six basic elements. It opens with a preamble that gives the benefits provided to the vassal by the suzerain and emphasizes the importance of exclusive loyalty by the vassal. Then follows a historical prologue describing the history of the relationship between the two powers. The next element describes the stipulations or the conditions on which the relation is based and then a provision for the treaty to be deposited in the Temple and periodically read in public. There usually follows a list of witnesses, which in the biblical covenant is often identified as "the heavens and the earth." There is finally a list of blessings and curses, the benefits of being faithful to the covenant and the negative consequences of failing to do so. The entire relationship is then ratified by a sacrifice that is intended to suggest the death of the covenant breaker. This implication explains the "sacrifice" in Genesis 15 when the Lord alone symbolically passes through the divided sacrifice animals thus pledging his own extinction if he fails to keep his promise to Abraham.

Quite obviously the covenant renewal lays special stress on the curses and blessings of the covenant in order to remind the participants of the consequences of either keeping or not keeping the commitments previously made. Since the Decalogue provided the basic requirements for Israel to maintain their relation to Yahweh, the repetition of the curses at Ebal/Gerizim were closely related to those ten words. What occurs here is not so much the giving of the law--that had occurred at Sinai--as it was "preaching" or exhortation to remember and observe the covenant relation.

Here we have an important insight into the nature of revelation. The close similarity of the biblical covenant with the suzerainty covenant pattern is a good example of how the Lord accommodates his revelation to mankind. In utilizing this covenant pattern God has taken something that is already understood as the starting point of a relationship. In a word, there is continuity between the historically conditioned understanding of the recipient and the divine disclosure. If there were total discontinuity, as some might like it to be, it would be incomprehensible. This fact is the basis for recovering the historical context in interpreting biblical passages as among the first steps in exegesis.

Love, the Basis of the Covenant

The call to covenant obedience should not be interpreted in a legalistic fashion because it is based on a Father-son relation characterized by love. Deuteronomy has been called the "biblical document *par excellence* of love." No book of the Old Testament is so shaped at every point by the suzerainty treaties to which we have made reference. If therefore there is any book of the Old Testament in which a love like that required of a vassal is likely to be found, it is in the book of

Deuteronomy. This type of covenant love is not sentimentality but primarily involves faithfulness and obedience such as is expressed in the father-son relationship characteristic of the patriarchal age. This characteristic is reflected in the fact that it was a love that could be commanded and therefore was more than an emotion. This point is clearly illustrated by the Shema (Deut. 6:5—"you shall love the Lord your God with all your heart, and with all your soul, and with all your might."), which is immediately followed with the words, "Keep these words that I am commanding you today in your heart" (v. 6). This whole history lies behind the words of Jesus, "If you love me, keep my commandments" (John 14:15).

One of the most theologically important truths about the covenant was that the covenant was established first and obedience followed. Thus the covenant was a free gift of grace from Yahweh and was not the result of any prior qualifications by good works or inherent value on Israel's part. Obedience was not a pre-condition of the covenant but the response to it. And furthermore the obedience involved was motivated by gratitude to the Lord for all he had done for his people and for his acceptance of them as his treasured possession (see Deut. 8:1ff; 9:1ff.).

The reaffirmation of the basic covenant relationship at Ebal/Gerizim is expressed in Deuteronomy 27:9-10—"Then Moses and the Levitical priests spoke to all Israel, saying: Keep silence and hear, O Israel! This very day you have become the people of the Lord your God. Therefore obey the Lord your God, observing his commandments and his statutes that I am commanding you today." This passage reflects the order just described: Israel's identity as God's people as the result of God grace and the lifestyle to which she is called in response.

Moses Prediction (Deut. 31:14-29)

In giving directions for the covenant renewal Moses made a dire prediction. The people would, in fact, fail to observe the covenant stipulations and thus suffer expulsion from the land. On what basis could God have instructed Moses to make this prediction? Certainly not determinism! Moses was a realist after having led these people for forty years. Only shortly after they had been delivered from the hand of Pharaoh they were worshipping a golden calf, an incident that the rabbis later identified as a recapitulation of Adam's sin and the fall of Israel. Repeatedly they had grumbled on the journey because life had become difficult. Thus knowing their weaknesses, their tendency to grumble and complain, the elderly leader could be sure that they would so violate the covenant that they would be cast out of the land (Deut. 30:1).

But there was good news! Moses declared that if they would return in penance to the Lord and change their ways, he would restore them to the land. Even more, he would address the issue that had been at the heart of their repeated failures and "circumcise your heart and the heart of your descendants, so that you will love the Lord your God with all your heart and with all your soul, in order that you may live" (vs. 6). This hopeful prophecy points us forward to the New Testament. In Romans 10:5-11 Paul picks up this Deuteronomic prediction of the end of exile and the accompanying inner transformation of the heart to declare that this development is precisely what has taken place in the Christ event.

Also, it is possible that Matthew has actually structured his Gospel to demonstrate that Jesus, in the Sermon on the Mount, is conducting a covenant renewal that embodies the fulfillment of Moses' "prophecy." It has become somewhat of a commonplace that Matthew organizes his material to conform to the five-fold pattern of the Pentateuch. Each of the five sections of the Gospel is marked by a similar phrase: "And it cam to pass when Jesus had finished . . ." (Matthew 7:28; 11:1; 13:53; 19:1; 26:1). This structure is not to be seen as corresponding to the sequence of the five books in the Pentateuch but the Pentateuch seen as *covenant*, and summarized as such at the end of it in Deuteronomy 27-30.

It is also possible that the first and last of these five units (cc. 5-7 and 23-25) serve as kind of bookends for this series of five sections. The first contains a series of nine blessings (the Beatitudes) and the last a series of seven "curses" expressed as "Woe to you, scribes and Pharisees." Setting these blessings and curses in parallel with each other has the effect of reproducing the covenant renewal at Mount Ebal/Gerizim.

If we accept this analysis, Matthew is picturing Jesus as a new Moses, conducting a covenant renewal that is a fulfillment of the prophecy of Moses that God would circumcise the heart thus making possible the righteousness that must exceed that of the scribes and Pharisees (Matthew 5:20). This implication further suggests that Matthew has woven this covenantal choice into the very structure of his gospel portraying it as the choice set before his contemporaries by Jesus, and thereby himself setting the same choice before the church of his own day. Matthew presupposes a telling of the Jewish story according to which Israel has failed, has ended in exile, and needs a new exodus; and he undertakes to show that this new exodus is now becoming a reality in the life, death and resurrection of Jesus. He is calling his readers—and us—to faithful covenant commitments.

Obedience and Success

The theology of Deuteronomy that is summarized in the covenant renewal at Ebal/Gerizim has sometimes been utilized to support the idea that obedience to God guarantees success in terms of health and prosperity. This inference is based on the fact that God promises the people success in the land if they obey and judgment if they do not, an inference that is often referred to as the "prosperity gospel." There are three interconnected reasons that invalidate this inference.

First, these are promises that are given to a particular people in a particular situation. The land was understood to be a gift to them from God, a gift with conditions. Continued residence in the land depended on their meeting these conditions, failure to do so would result in expulsion and exile. Generalizing these circumstances to refer to a general promise of prosperity or health conditioned on faith or obedience would be a faulty interpretive move. Second, the purpose for the gift of the land was missional. Israel's election involved their responsibility to embody what it meant for humans to live out the implications of having been created in the image of God. We have seen that an aspect of that image was a relation of stewardship to the land. Thus the gift of the land was not primarily for their own benefit but for them to demonstrate to others how God intended humans to manifest environmental responsibility. Third, the land was a corporate gift in the sense that every family had an inheritance that was to remain theirs in perpetuity. While hardship might force them to temporarily transfer property to another, there was never a permanent sale. As yet, there is no archeological evidence of Israelite sale and purchase of land, though there are many such transactions in Canaanite culture. In addition to this evidence, there is not even a provision in the Old Testament for the sale of land. Land could not be transferred except to heirs.

Furthermore, there was the provision for the year of Jubilee every fifty years when all land would to be returned to its original owner and all debts cancelled. This event entailed a "redistribution of wealth." This provision was apparently designed to prohibit the accumulation of wealth in the hands of a few, which would be the practical consequence of a "prosperity gospel." That there is no evidence that Israel ever observed the Jubilee provision suggests the self-centered nature of the so-called "prosperity gospel".

This analysis does not imply that it is sinful to acquire wealth. John Wesley admitted that he unintentionally became wealthy but most of it he gave away. The work of the Kingdom would clearly suffer if it were not for the generous support of those whom God has blessed with a measure of financial success. The issue with the contemporary Christian, like that of ancient Israel, is the challenge to exercise responsible and judicial stewardship of ones possessions.

Reflections

All intimate relations need repeated efforts to maintain the level of intimacy that characterized the initial relation. Otherwise the result will likely be as John the Revelator described in addressing the church at Ephesus where Jesus says: "I have this against you, that you have abandoned the love you had at first" (Revelation 2:4).

Occasionally married couples will have a ceremony in which they repeat their vows, thus renewing their dedication to each other. This practice is similar to what is going on with Israel at Mount Ebal/Gerizim. She is being invited to recall the events that brought her unto existence as a nation and recommit herself to the exclusive worship and service of the Lord.

Each new era in the life of the people of God calls for a renewed commitment to keep God first and recognize the implications of that commitment for the new circumstances. In Israel's case they were entering an untried way of life and much of Deuteronomy spells out how their relation to God is to manifest itself in that context. This reason explains why there are numerous instructions regarding how they are to relate to the land and its products. Historically, they had been shepherds rather than farmers. Tilling the soil and raising crops was to be a new experience.

For this reason, Deuteronomy is dominated from the beginning to end by the idea of the land that they are now entering. The commandments restated by Moses have no other purpose in view than that of laying down the new style of worship and the new way of life for the radically altered circumstances arising from living a settled existence on the land. Repeatedly he says, "When you come into the land which Yahweh your God gives to you, then you shall . . . ."

While humanity's relation to the "earth" or "land" is one aspect of the image of God, in the contemporary situation life is no longer as *directly* related to the soil as with Israel in Palestine. Furthermore, by the time of Jesus as well as the result of his work, the idea of the "land" has been enlarged from referring to a small strip of real estate by the Mediterranean Sea to include the whole world (see Matthew 5:5). Urban society with its innumerable apartment dwellers would have difficulty relating the biblical injunctions about agricultural life to their setting. Here is a new situation that calls for a different sort of stewardship. Christopher Wright highlights the clue to this situation: "All that we can count as material goods originates from what grows on, feeds on, or is dug out of the soil of our planet."[18] Although this observation does not relieve God's people from environmental responsibility, it does point to the fact that the theology of the covenant responsibilities regarding the land should now be applied to all possessions.

John Wesley spells out the implications of this stewardship with the principle that "if you do not spend your money in doing good to others, you must spend it to the hurt of yourself." He elaborates the principle: "If we waste our money, we are not only guilty of wasting a talent which God has given us, but we do ourselves the farther [sic] harm, we turn this useful talent into a powerful means of corrupting ourselves; because so far as it is spent wrong, so far it is spent in the support of some wrong temper, in gratifying some vain and unreasonable desires, which, as Christians, we are obliged to renounce."[19]

Wesley's advice on the use of money partly reflects his understanding of how the Christian is to reflect the image of God. This advice is expressed in terms of three brief rules: (1) make all you can, (2) save all you can and (3) give all you can. These are elaborated in his sermon on "The Use of Money." We should make all we can without hurting ourselves or our neighbor and always within the bounds of honesty and legality. The second rule enjoins simplicity of lifestyle as a way of avoiding extravagance to satisfy our personal desires and to glorify God rather than building up a large bank account. The third is elaborated by some prudential guidelines:

---

[18]Christopher J. H. Wright, *God's People in God's Land* (Grand Rapids: Wm. B. Eerdmans Pub., 1990), 3.
[19]*Works*, 5:374.

> If you desire to be a 'faithful and wise steward,' out of that portion of your Lord's good which he has for the present lodged in your hands, but with the right of resumption whenever it pleaseth him, (1) Provide things needful for yourself; food to eat, raiment to put on; whatever nature moderately requires, for preserving you both in health and strength. (2) Provide these for your wife, your children, your servants, or any others who pertain to your household. If when this is done, there is an overplus left, then do good to 'them that are of the household of faith.' If there be an overplus still, 'as you have opportunity, do good unto all men.' In so doing, you *give all you can*; nay, in a sound sense, all you have.[20]

For about 12 years following retirement, we lived in a small house near a major lake. My son and I had constructed it prior to retiring, including building a masonry fireplace. During the winter months, especially when there happened to be a snow on the ground, we really enjoyed the cozy comfort of sitting by the fire playing board games and drinking hot chocolate. But it involved a lot of work and attention since the tendency of fire is to go out. We had to be continually adding firewood, which had to be cut and often split.

The spiritual life is quite similar to our experience with the fireplace. St. Paul recognized this character and urged his converts to "maintain the spiritual glow" (Romans 12:11, Moffatt). The fire of the Spirit needs constant feeding and attention. There may be times when it burns low and the fuel needs to be replenished.

While it may seem mundane, this renewal is one of the chief benefits of regular attendance at public worship. Those who analyze such matters tell us that for young adults these days, regular church attendance means one or two Sundays a month. The sad fact is that a fire that burns too low is likely to go out. No doubt the Hebrews' author had this in mind when he (or she) exhorted his readers to "forsake not the assembling of yourselves together" (10:25, KJV). Just as a single log in the fireplace doesn't burn well, the believer's experience is strengthened and enhanced by the faith of others.

It occurs to me that there is another related analogy with maintaining the fire. If we keep stoking the old fuel, it will eventually

---

[20]Ibid. 7:10.

turn to dead ashes. The result is no heat. New wood on the fire is essential. This suggests the importance of a continual pursuit of an ever-deeper understanding of the faith. People who simply keep "warming over" old ideas without ever being challenged and excited by new truth tend to get bored. And boredom results in apathy and apathy results in dying embers.

Thus, the significance of covenant renewal experiences! They may take different forms but they are necessary to keep the fire blazing in our "fireplace" of commitment to and love for God. Lovers who are apart keep their love alive through letters. When one arrives, the recipient devours its contents and scours it repeatedly for evidences of love. In a sense, God has written us a love letter in anticipation of the time when the "engaged couple" will be united in marriage. Scouring that letter will maintain our enthusiasm until the time when the "new Jerusalem" ("the bride adorned for her husband") comes to earth in final consummation (Revelation 21:2).

Questions to Think About:
1. What rituals do Christians observe that can function as covenant renewal ceremonies?
2. Since "revival meetings" seem to no longer be very effective means of evangelism, can they retain their significance as a means of covenant renewal?
3. What does the aspect of the image of God relating to the earth imply for the Christian's attitude toward global warming?
4. Do you think the Christian should view financial success as a reward for righteous living?

Chapter Five

MOUNT ZION

The Revelation of God's Presence Among His People

When Solomon had ended his prayer, fire came down from heaven and consumed the burnt offering and the sacrifices; and the glory of the Lord filled the temple. The priests could not enter the house of the Lord, because the glory of the Lord filled the Lord's house. When all the people of Israel saw the fire come down and the glory of the Lord on the temple, they bowed down on the pavement with their faces to the ground, and worshipped and gave thanks to the Lord, saying, "For he is good, for his steadfast love endures forever" (2 Chron. 7:1-3).

Mount Zion

There is no abstract Hebrew word corresponding to the English word "presence." The term most often translated into English as "presence" is the word for "face." This is why Genesis 3:8 literally describes the result of the first pair's violating the prohibition against eating the forbidden fruit as hiding themselves from "face of the Lord." Fear and guilt resulted from violating the integrity of their relation to the Creator. It is fair to suggest that to be in the presence of God is the same as being in right relation to Him. This relationship is theologically significant since one aspect of humanity's creation in the image of God is a special relation to God. Before the disruption of the relation of the first pair with the Creator, their situation can really be described as a face-to-face relation in which they could "look God in the eye" without guilt or fear.

God's Presence Crucial

For the people of Israel who were constituted a "holy nation" by way of the Sinai covenant, the "presence of God" was essential for their survival and existence as a body. From the beginning of their life as a "delivered" people, God had often manifested his presence both to them and on their behalf. In those precarious moments on the shore of the Red Sea, it was the presence of God visible in the cloud of fire and smoke that provided protection from the army of Pharaoh. After crossing the Sea, that cloud guided them through the wilderness.

When Isaiah pictured the "new exodus" from the Babylonian captivity, he used the imagery of the "cloudy pillar" from the original exodus: "For you shall not go out in haste, and you shall not go in flight; for the Lord will go before you, and the God of Israel will be your rear guard (Isa. 52:12). The metaphor is the same but the whole atmosphere is different. Instead of being pursued from behind ("go out in haste") they will be drawn by a glorious future rather than being driven by a threatening past. In either case it is God's presence that always guides and protects them.

As important as it was for their existence and purpose, God's presence with his people was not automatic or unconditional. The aftermath of the golden calf incident dramatically demonstrated its conditional nature. Because of their idolatry, God proposed to send the people on their way to the Promised Land but declined to go with them, sending an angel instead (Ex. 33:2-3). Knowing that there was no substitute for God's presence, in desperation Moses entered the tent of meeting and interceded with the Lord on behalf of the people, appealing to his own relation to God: "If your presence will not go, do not carry us up from here. For how shall it be known that I have found favor in your sight, I and your people, unless you go with us? In this way, we shall be distinct, I and your people, from every people on the face of the earth" (Ex. 33:15-16). Moses knew that it was the divine presence that made Israel the people of the Lord, not blood or soil. With God they were invincible, and without him they were just another peasant nation without a particular uniqueness or secure future.

After entrance into the land of promise, the presence of God tended to occupy only a peripheral and sometimes ambiguous relation to the national life of the people. This situation resulted in one of the darkest periods of their history (see the book of Judges and early First Samuel). The situation changed (at least externally) during the reign of David when he acquired Jerusalem as his capital city and relocated the Ark of the Covenant there. Out of his dream to provide God a permanent dwelling place at the heart of the nation, provision was made to build a Temple, the construction of which became the task of David's son, Solomon. Upon its cleansing and dedication, the glory of God pervaded the now sacred precincts, whereupon the Temple became the symbol and heart of Israel's religion, a concrete sign that God was present in the midst of his people.

The Role of the Temple

Solomon's prayer of dedication recognized that God could not be confined to one location nor does he need a building. So, theoretically, the rationale for the Temple was not to domesticate God to a specific spot, although that became the outcome. The ideal reason is doubtless because humanity needs some visible thing by which to realize God's loving presence. In time the Temple became the central symbol of Judaism, the location of Israel's most characteristic practice, the topic of some of her most vital stories, the answer to her deepest questions, and the subject of some of her most beautiful songs.

In addition to the earthly dwelling place of God, the Temple was the place of sacrifice, which was the means of sustaining the people's relation to God. It also had great political significance, as was quite obvious in Jesus' day. But Solomon's insight into the conditional nature of the Divine presence that informed his prayer ultimately became reality. In the course of time the failure of the people to keep the worship of Yahweh at the center of their personal and national lives led to the departure of the divine presence from the Temple. The developments that led to this result stand at the heart of the prophetic message of Isaiah, Jeremiah and Ezekiel.

By the time of Jeremiah in the seventh century B.C. the people had come to think of the Temple as a magical charm to ward off judgment. Since, they reasoned, the Temple was the dwelling place of God, it would preserve both itself and the city of Jerusalem inviolate in spite of the wayward moral lives of the people. Jeremiah, at the risk of his own life, attacked this perverted concept of God's presence. In Jeremiah 7:4 he declared, "do not trust in these deceptive words: 'This is the temple of the Lord, the temple of the Lord, the temple of the Lord'."

In contrast to this ancient version of "unconditional eternal security," the prophet said to the people, "For if you truly amend your ways and your doing, if you truly act justly one with another, if you do not oppress the alien, the orphan, and the widow, or shed innocent blood in this place, and if you do not go after other gods to your own hurt, then I will dwell with you in this place, in the land that I gave of old to your ancestors forever and ever" (Jer. 7:5-7). But these words fell on deaf ears resulting not in repentance but in persecution of the prophet (see Jer. 26). We see this same scenario reflected in the message of Jesus as he warned Israel to abandon their way of violent revolution and follow his way of peace. No doubt, this emphasis is why some of the people identified him as Jeremiah returned. The response of the Temple officials ultimately led to his death.

The Departure of the Glory

Although among the captives who had been carried away to Babylon in the first deportation, Ezekiel was granted visions of how the situation in Jerusalem had gone from bad to worse. In the midst of the constantly deteriorating moral condition of both priests and people, the prophet received a vision that was to him, as a priest, devastating. He saw the inevitable outcome of the downward course of Judah, the departure of the *Shekinah* from the Temple. Gone would be the presence and glory of God!

Ezekiel's call to be a prophet took the form of a vision of the "glory of the Lord," a vision that involved a number of strange features. That dramatic and fascinating vision constituted the unifying element of the book containing his work and messages. In Ezekiel 9:3, he sees the "glory" remove itself from its normal abode in the Holy of Holies to the threshold of the Temple: "Now the glory of the God of Israel had gone up from the cherub on which it rested to the threshold of the house." Soon he sees it once again lift and further remove itself from this intermediate location: "Then the glory of the Lord went out from the threshold of the house and stopped above the cherubim. The cherubim lifted up their wings and rose up from the earth in my sight as they went out with the wheels beside them. They stopped at the entrance of the east gate of the house of the Lord; and the glory of the God of Israel was above them" (10:18-19). Finally the presence of God abandoned the city itself, pausing on the surrounding mountain east of the city (11:22), evidently facing toward Babylon where the exiles had been carried. At this juncture of his ministry, Ezekiel turned to the future and envisioned both the rebuilding of the Temple and the return of the glory ushering in a golden age. (See chapter 7)

This series of visions gives one the impression of reluctance, like a dove whose owner had deliberately injured it with the result that it was unable to remain because of its rejection and sadly departed. Although God was not eager to withdraw his presence, the continued rebellion and disobedience of Judah had grieved his heart and left him no alternative. The end result was the destruction of the city and Temple in 587 B.C. demonstrating that the presence of the Lord was indeed the guarantee of his people's protection, but not unconditionally.

A Disappointed Hope

With the end of the physical captivity when Babylon was defeated and Cyrus the Persian became ruler, the people who returned to Palestine did so with the hope that Ezekiel's visions would be fulfilled. The first item on their agenda was the restoration of the Temple. Ultimately, a Temple was built but the glory did not return, resulting in renewed disillusionment. They were still under pagan domination and, apart from a short interlude under the Maccabees, remained so until the time of Jesus.

Thus, the dominant mood of the Jews in the first century B.C. was that the exile had never ended. However, they were still being sustained by the hope that God would return to his people, deliver them from domination by the pagans, and establish the kingdom of God. This hope was a major theme of the post-exilic prophets. Malachi, in particular, had predicted that God's return to his people would occur: "See, I am sending my messenger to prepare the way before me, and the Lord whom you seek will suddenly come to his temple. The messenger of the covenant in whom you delight—indeed, he is coming says the Lord of hosts. But who can endure the day of his coming, and who can stand when he appears?" (Mal. 3:1-2a)

The Temple Replaced

Both in his teaching and his practice, Jesus indicated that the prophecy of Malachi was being fulfilled by his own presence. But his vocation was so marked by anomalies from the prevailing understanding that it ran drastically counter to the prevailing worldview. Ultimately, a new understanding had to radically transform the expectations that dominated

Second Temple Judaism. For our purposes here, one of those transformations involved a reorientation of the hope for the presence of God returning to the Temple.

The Temple was of immense importance in first-century Judaism both religiously and politically, but its leadership had become corrupt. More than one group of Jews had disassociated themselves from the Temple for that reason, even though they ordered their understanding of human purity and divine holiness in ways embodied in the architecture of the Temple. The Qumran community is the most familiar example of such separationists. Jesus, both in his teaching and action, like Jeremiah, implicitly prophesied the destruction of the Temple along with the nation itself. This meaning is the essence of the so-called apocalyptic passages in Mark 13 (par. Matt. 24: 1-8; Luke 25:1-11) that modern pop prophecy has mistakenly insisted relates to the end of the world and the second coming of Christ. The early and classic Wesleyan commentary by Adam Clarke supported a more correct interpretation, as have the best of biblical scholars since.

Several events during the final days of the ministry of Jesus signaled the end of the Temple as representative of the presence of God. The most notable one was his "cleansing" of the Temple by disrupting the activity of the money-changers (Mark 11:15-19; Matt. 21:12-17; Luke 19:45-48; John 2:13-22). There were several implications of this action, including its being the proximate cause of his arrest, trial, and execution. Several scholars have pointed out that the Temple, its structure and its organization, had become the basis for a social way of life characterized by the domination of the "have nots" by the "haves," both economically and politically. Thus, Jesus was challenging the position and privileges of the Temple elite.

More importantly, He was interrupting one of the most significant functions of the Temple. Since the money-changers were making available the Temple tax with which the worshipper could purchase qualified animals for sacrifice, this action at least temporarily suspended the sacrifices and without sacrifice the Temple had lost its whole reason for being. It was thus a symbolic action that was an indication of the destruction of the entire Temple system and, by implication, that an alternate form of dealing with the sin problem was in the offing.

The last meal Jesus shared with his disciples signaled a similar message. Jesus was substituting his own death for the sacrifices of the Temple, symbolized by the bread and wine. The Temple-action and the Last Supper, taken together, indicated that Jesus was in effect intending to replace the Temple as the heart of Judaism with his own newly instituted cultic meal. No doubt Jesus' observance of the "Passover" at the "wrong" time had the same significance. He was precisely not keeping it as simply one more in a sequence of subversive acts. He celebrated the Passover at the time of the slaughter of the lambs for the sacrifice in the Temple suggesting that he is now to become the sacrificial lamb. Jesus was implicitly demonstrating that in his approaching death he was bringing the long-anticipated restoration of the presence of God to its intended climax.

Another sign that Jesus' death signaled the end of the Jerusalem Temple as the locus of the presence of God was the reference in Mark 15:38. When Jesus breathed his last, "the curtain of the temple was torn in two, from top to bottom." Thus, with the death of Jesus the Temple is symbolically destroyed. It is of considerable interest that several Jewish texts composed before 70 A.D. announce that the old Temple will not continue into the new age. God will instead build a new one. While clearly having a different meaning in view, this belief directs our attention to the enigmatic words of Jesus that perplexed those Temple authorities who heard it and became a source of derision: "Destroy this temple and in three days I will raise it up" (Jn. 2:19).

Thus, from the Christian perspective, the presence of God is now to be found, not in a building no matter how sacred, but embodied in a person, the person of the crucified and risen Messiah and with those who by faith are identified with him. This truth is implied by the descent of the dove at Jesus' baptism reflecting a reversal of the departure of the "glory" from Solomon's Temple in Ezekiel's vision. Thus Jesus himself became the locus of the presence of God, in a word the new Temple.

A subsidiary but equally important transition was also taking place. Within Second Temple Judaism the Torah had assumed new importance in the border territory, as in Galilee, and acquired some of the functions and attributes of the Temple itself. Thus it too came to be viewed as an incarnation of the presence of God. This belief is reflected in the following statement of the *Mishnah*: "If two [persons] sit together and words of the Law [are spoken] between them, the Divine Presence rests between them." We have no difficulty recognizing the transformation of the locus of the Shekinah when Jesus assures his followers that "where 2 or 3 are gathered in my name, there am I in the midst" (Matt. 18:20).

This discussion calls our attention to a major element in the Old Testament understanding of the presence of God as represented by the tabernacle and then the Temple. It was the aspect of Israel's religion that symbolized the unity of the people. In the instructions for the encampment given to Moses, the tribes were located in a symmetrical pattern with the tabernacle at the center so that all were related together by their proximity to the presence of God. After the destruction of the Temple in 587 B.C. the eschatological hope for a new Temple shared the same vision. The sanctuary would be the central and unifying factor of Israelite life in the new age.

The same significance is attached to the Divine presence as embodied in Jesus the Messiah. It is why Paul is so insistent on the importance of the unity of the church. That unity is not to be found in cultural or ethnic characteristics but in the fact that all believers are one is Christ. That unity transcends all merely human qualities so that, as the Apostle could emphasize more than once, "in Christ" there is neither Jew nor Greek, bond nor free, male nor female, but all are one in Christ (Rom. 10:12; Gal. 3:28; Col. 3:11).

God's Presence Today

God manifested his presence with Israel in her early days through physical phenomena. This fact reflects the significance of the term "glory" (Heb. doxa), which is a technical term for God's accommodation to human limitations by manifesting himself in visible form, such as the burning bush. This sign made it relatively easy to determine that God was in fact among his people. Now that the locus of God's presence has become centered in Jesus Christ and the people who are in relation to him, are there evidences that can be identified, ways by which we can determine that God is with us? Since the presence of God is now to be recognized as the work of the Holy Spirit, the question is really, how do we recognize the presence of the Holy Spirit?

The answer to that question is at least partially addressed in the Upper Room discourses of Jesus found in the Gospel of John. Jesus' description of the promised Comforter (Paraclete) demonstrates an intimate relation between the Spirit and himself. Several parallels are drawn between the Paraclete (Spirit) and Jesus: (1) both Jesus and the Spirit are sent by the Father (Jn. 5:43;15:26); (2) the Spirit is described as *another* Paraclete, meaning that Jesus is the first (Jn. 14:16; (3) the reference to the Paraclete as the "Spirit of Truth" (14:17) corresponds to Jesus as the Truth (14:6); (4) as the disciples recognized Jesus (14:7, 9) so also will they recognize the Paraclete (14:17); (5) if the world will not receive Jesus, neither will it receive the Paraclete (14:17); (6) and the Spirit will continue Jesus' ministry (16:8-11).

The bottom line is that the Holy Spirit given at Jesus' glorification (Jn. 7:39) will manifest the character of Jesus and speak of Jesus and not of himself. The Spirit, his character and work as the presence of God among and within God's people, will conform to a Christ-like criterion. What is true of John's report is also true of Paul's theology of the Spirit. Jesus and the Spirit are so intimately related in Paul that some scholars have suggested that for the Apostle they were identical (e.g., 2 Cor. 3:17). Although this conclusion is unacceptable—they are different "persons" of the one Trinity of God's being--it is clearly true that Paul's view of the Spirit is essentially Christocentric. He typically portrays the Spirit as an actor who has become so absorbed in his role and plays it so skillfully that we forget the actor, who becomes for us the person being portraying.

In evaluating Paul's contribution to the understanding of the Holy Spirit, James S. Stewart says:

> In the primitive Christian community there was a tendency at the first—perhaps quite natural under the circumstances—to revert to the cruder conceptions of the Spirit, and to trace His working mainly in such phenomena as speaking with tongues. It was Paul who saved the nascent faith from that dangerous retrogression. Not in any accidental and extraneous phenomena, he insisted, not in any spasmodic emotions or intermittent ecstasies were the real token of God's Spirit to be found, but in the quiet, stead, normal life of faith, in power that worked on moral levels, in the soul's secret inward assurance of its sonship of God, in love and joy and peace and patience and *a character like that of Jesus.*[21]

These observations give us a clue to a possible answer to several important questions regarding the nature and function of the Spirit. William Barclay begins his book about the Holy Spirit by noting that our thinking about the Spirit is vaguer and more undefined than our thinking about any other part of the Christian faith. One major reason for this vagueness is the difficulty of thinking about the reality of

---

[21]James S. Stewart, *A Man in Christ* (N.Y.: Harper and Row, Pub., n.d.), 308. Emphasis added.

"spirit." It may be that the average person probably thinks about the Holy Spirit as a quasi-material entity like "Casper the ghost." And this awkwardness may be exacerbated by the *King James Version* translation of *pneuma* as "Ghost." We may be tempted to think about the Holy Spirit as one among several "spirits" having actual reality, although the Holy Spirit may be the most distinctive of them all. One thing that contributes to this confusion is the emphasis of conservative theologians that the Holy Spirit is a "person." It would probably be sounder in today's setting to speak of the Spirit as "personal" since the modern meaning of "person" refers to an "individual person." By contrast, the ancient meaning was relational. Whereas the concept of an "individual" emphasizes separate self-sufficiency, a "person" is one who, like the Father, Son, and Holy Spirit, has his or her being in relationships.

The most influential and generally accepted theological interpretation of the Holy Spirit supports this interpretation. It was expressed by St. Augustine long ago. The Father is father in relation to the Son; the Son is son in relation to the Father and the Holy Spirit is the bond of unity between Father and Son on the one hand, and between God and believers on the other. The Holy Spirit forges bonds of unity between believers, upon which the unity of the church ultimately depends. Since the church is the "temple of the Holy Spirit," within which the Holy Spirit dwells, the same Spirit that binds together the Father and Son in the unity of the Godhead also binds together believers in the unity of the church.

As with ancient Israel, so with today's church. As the Divine presence is the source of the unity of the church, the evidence of the presence and ministry of the Spirit is that unity. The absence of unity is evidence of the absence of the Spirit. This fact is why Paul is so concerned for this issue and why those who understand its crucial significance place so much stress on a unity as reflected in the popular aphorism, "In essentials unity, in non-essentials liberty, and in all things charity."

The Spirit functions for the church as the cloud and fire representing God's presence functioned for Israel. He gives guidance in the church's pilgrimage from the "New Exodus" (Jesus' Resurrection) to the final consummation. The Spirit is the strange, personal presence of the living God himself, leading, guiding, warning, rebuking, grieving over our failings and celebrating our small steps toward the true inheritance.

Each of these functions can be distorted by failing to test them by the Christ-pattern. Apart from this point of reference it is extremely difficult to distinguish one's own desires or cultural influences from an authentic influence of divine origin. Many manifestations that claim to be initiated by the Spirit cannot be accounted as genuine by the Christ-like criteria. Paul is evidently appealing to this test in his response to the problems of the Corinthian church.

This analysis highlights the importance for the Christian believer who desires to be sensitive to the guidance and activity of the Spirit of being a diligent student of God's word. This implication is, in part, the basis for both Paul and Peter urging believers to grow in knowledge as the essential basis for growing in grace, which is growth in Christ-likeness (cf. 2 Pet. 3:18).

One clue to thinking biblically about the Holy Spirit is to focus on the fact that in the New Testament the Holy Spirit is primarily a corporate gift but derivatively a personal one. In Acts, the bestowment of the Spirit is given to groups and not to an individual as individual. The two possible exceptions are Saul of Tarsus and Apollo. Though an individual, Saul only received the Spirit when the church came to him in the person of Ananias. The text (Acts 18:24-28) does not mention Apollo receiving the Spirit although it may be implied by being paired by Luke with the incident of the 12 Ephesian disciples. Aquila and Priscilla would be the representatives of the church in that case. Paul expressly emphasizes both dimensions in 1 Corinthians 3:16 (corporate) and 6:19 (personal).

When believers gather in his name, Jesus promised to be present. How is he present? He is present in the form of the Holy Spirit of whom, as a worshipping community, we ideally become aware as heaven and earth, God's realm and the earthly realm, interconnect and interlock. This intersection comes about through hymn, prayer, sacrament, and word. It transcends the kind of "spirit" that is present in a musical concert designed for entertainment or generated by various kinds of psychological stimuli. It occurs as the result of the corporate response to the reality of who God is and what God has done on our behalf and is now doing in our lives.

When as individuals we depart from this corporate encounter with the Spirit in the awareness that the Lord was present, we carry this "Spirit" with us—or better, the Spirit carries us. But unless we foster this sense of divine presence by involvement with the "body," it may begin to fade. That is why the writer to the Hebrews warned against failing to gather to worship with the saints (10:25). It is the principle analogous to the physical fact that a single log blazing in the fireplace tends to go out. This principle illustrates that the presence of the Holy Spirit is primarily corporate in nature, with the personal dimension being derivative from the environment of the church, the body of Christ.

REFLECTIONS

The biblical teaching about the presence of God raises many questions for contemporary Christians. Such questions are especially crucial for sincere believers who are critically aware of the subtle intrusion of subjective factors in matters like divine guidance and proposed evidences of God's presence. We all know that if God is God, he is present everywhere. However, this intellectual awareness of God's so-called "omnipresence" is not enough. We want to know that God is present in a special way in certain situations. One of those situations is the setting of public worship. We usually open our service with a prayer of "invocation," in which we invite God to come. However, we really know that God is already there so the proper purpose of such a prayer is actually for ourselves. We wish to become sensitively aware that God is among us.

In my own denominational tradition, the recognized founder, Phineas F. Bresee, was famous for his repeated exhortation to his congregation to "keep the glory down." Before passing away he went from camp meeting to camp meeting, from revival to revival, exhorting his audience to keep the glory down. He would say, we may be whipped to pieces if our doctrine is attacked; we may not be theologically correct in everything, but we have the glory and the power and the anointing of God, and whatever you do, don't lose it or you'll have nothing.

What did he mean by "the glory?" When you read the history, it is clear that the "glory" among the early followers of Bresee was thought to be accompanied or manifested by physical manifestations such as "shouting," "waving of a handkerchief," the raising of hands in praise. However, it is equally clear that such demonstration was understood to be in response to truth and not simply emotionalism. Bresee was very clear that such demonstration should not happen until *after* the sermon had been preached. "Getting the glory down" was never a substitute for the preaching of the Word. It must be a *response* to the preaching of the Word. On one occasion when one of his leading members anticipated the climax of the sermon and got up and started getting very emotional while he was still preaching, he said, "not yet, brother Gay, not yet."

Many preachers subsequently mistakenly identified the demonstrations with the "glory" and sought to generate a response by artificial means. The result was hollowness. What they failed to recognize was that those early responses, while genuine and real, were culturally conditioned. With cultural changes, responses to God's presence take a different form of expression. The enduring characteristic of God's presence is love, compassion, integrity and increasing conformity to the image of God as embodied in Jesus Christ.

Throughout my long ministry, I have encountered many claims for divine guidance. Denominational leaders have sought to sustain their positions by claiming that God gave them the plan. A few have defended positions contrary to the Word based on a personal revelation. More than one young person has professed a call to preacher when gifts for such a vocation were totally absent. I have concluded that relatively certain knowledge of the validity of divine guidance is the result of hindsight. Sometimes we have to take a step of faith in order to verify that we have rightly interpreted what we think to be God's direction and history will either validate or invalidate its authenticity. It has worked for me!

Questions to Think About
1. How would you evaluate the authenticity of any exercise of "spiritual gifts?"
2. What is the fallacy being expressed by persons who claim they are Christian but do not need the church?
3. What suggestions would you make to a congregation to enhance God's active presence among them?
4. How should we test the phenomenon of "divine guidance" for authenticity?
5. When, where, and what is the temple of God today, the place of God's assured presence?

Chapter Six

MOUNT CARMEL

Revelation of the Sovereignty of God

At the time of the offering of the oblation, the prophet Elijah came near and said, "O Lord, God of Abraham, Isaac, and Israel, let it be known this day that you are God in Israel, that I am your servant, and that I have done all these things at your bidding. Answer me, O Lord, answer me, so that this people may know that you, O Lord, are God, and that you have turned their hearts back." Then the fire of the Lord fell and consumed the burnt offering, the wood, the stones, and the dust, and even licked up the water that was in the trench. When all the people saw it, they fell on their faces and said, "The Lord indeed is God; the Lord indeed is God" (1 Kings 18:36-39).

Mount Carmel

The one event I remember from my Cub Scout days was a field trip to a lakeside site. In the evening we joined the Boy Scouts around a campfire. The only thing about it that I recall was at the very beginning. When we arrived it was so dark that we could barely see. We were arranged in a semi-circle when suddenly, as if out of the sky, a flame appeared and descended into the center of the group igniting the campfire. We were all duly impressed.

This dramatic event came to mind as I thought about the events that took place on Mount Carmel. The prophet Elijah had challenged the prophets of Baal to a contest to determine who would be the official deity of Israel. The outcome was to be based on which god answered by fire. My experience as a Cub Scout was contrived and easily explained, but Elijah's was one of the most spectacular manifestations of God's power recorded anywhere in the Old Testament.

Mount Carmel is a range of mountains extending from the central highlands of Palestine to the shore of the Mediterranean Sea. It is impossible to identify the precise spot where the celebrated contest between Elijah and the prophets of Baal took place, but certain aspects of the narrative indicate the presence of water. This aspect suggests the point of the range shown in the picture near the Sea close to the present city of Haifa.

But if the place cannot be determined with certainty, the issue at stake was very clear and extremely important. This event in the northern kingdom of Israel was somewhat of a climax in the troubling encounter between Yahweh and Baalism that had been present from the first entrance of Israel into the Promised Land. Who, indeed, is actually God? Who is truly sovereign over all of creation? Who alone is worthy of being worshipped by Israel?

The Dramatic Confrontation

The descendents of Abraham had been herdsmen of sheep and cattle for all of their history. Even in their settled life in Egypt that form of life was never abandoned or forgotten. They knew how to care for their animals and they were aware that Yahweh could make their flocks multiply. But, when they contemplated entering the Promised Land, they were facing an agricultural way of life with which they were quite unfamiliar. It posed a double challenge to them.

The issue involved more than effective farming methods. Fundamentally, it involved a religious dimension as did virtually all activities in the ancient world. There was an inseparable relation between the dominant Canaanite religion and the productivity of the soil. The god of this religion was named Baal, who had a consort (wife) named Ashtoreth. The nature of Baal worship was, like all fertility religions, sexual in orientation. Baal worshippers assumed that he was responsible for making the soil fruitful--and from all appearances, it appeared to be successful. Thus, there was an overwhelming perennial temptation, as in all ages and for all people, for the Israelites to worship the "god of success." In addition, since the worship of Baal was accompanied by sexual activity to stimulate him to be active--both male and female prostitutes populated the shrines--this aspect offered a further temptation to Israel to compromise their exclusive love of and loyalty to Yahweh and his ethical standards.

The matter reached near disastrous proportions in the northern kingdom of Israel during the ninth century B.C. King Omri and his son Ahab created an alliance with Phoenicia that was sealed by the marriage of young Ahab to the daughter of the king of Tyre (1 Kings 16:31), the notorious Jezebel. Not only did Ahab allow her to have a temple to Baal built in the capital of Samaria, but she proceeded with missionary zeal to attempt to make Baalism the official religion of Israel.

John Bright describes the seriousness of this situation: "Yahweh had called [Israel], entered into covenant with her, summoned her to live in obedience to his righteous law, and given her a sense of destiny as his people. Baal, on the contrary, would have been destructive of the very faith that made Israel what she was.... Had Israel embraced Baal it would have been the end of her; she would no longer have lived as the peculiar people of God. Not one scrap of her heritage would have survived."[22]

While most of the prophets had capitulated under the intense pressure, a few took on the sometimes perilous task of being champions of Yahweh and countering this dire threat. Elijah was the most prominent of these. In the name of the God of Israel, this faithful prophet declared holy war on Ahab and his pagan state, queen and pagan god. It was in this context that the fiery prophet challenged the prophets of Baal to a contest to determine who would be the state god of Israel, Yahweh or Baal.

In one of the best known and most dramatic scenes in the Old Testament the entourage gathered on Mt. Carmel. The outcome of the contest was to be settled by which deity would "answer by fire." There is little need to retell the account since it is so familiar to Bible readers. But one wonders how many believers today would be willing to put their faith to such a meteorological test. However, there may be other ways by which faith can be put to a test.

Average Bible readers seldom ask questions about what happened. We certainly do not think of it as occurring like my experience as a cub scout. Clearly, if such deceptions were available, the prophets of Baal would have been privy to them. The soaking of Elijah's offering with

---

[22]John Bright, *The Kingdom of God* (N.Y.: Abingdon Press, 1953), 53.

water suggests that such deceptions were known and the prophet wanted to avoid that accusation. However, biblical scholars, both liberal and conservative, do raise questions about what happened. There is strong agreement among both that the "fire from heaven" may have been lightning. There were Old Testament precedents providing justification for this suggestion (Lev. 9:23-24). One was in a situation with similar issues (1 Sam. 7:3-11). If one keeps in mind that what we might call a "miracle" can, and often does, involve an appropriate timing rather than a violation of the normal processes of nature, we might consider lightning a possibility.

The difficulty here is that the sky was cloudless. The drought had not yet been broken and it was only after the triumph over the prophets of Baal that Elijah's servant saw the first fragment of a cloud on the far horizon. Had the sky been full of thunderclouds, it would still have been a remarkable vindication of Elijah's faith that the flash of lightning fell just at that moment and that it struck his altar and not the altar of Baal. But a flash from a cloudless sky must have seemed even more remarkable. Indeed, it would seem remarkable to us, and it is not to be supposed that we have rationalized the story and explained miracle away when we think in terms of a flash of lightning as God's means of answering Elijah's prayer.

Not only are there meteorological aspects to this event, but other facets of the contest also have interesting theological implications. It is not insignificant that Baal was supposed to be sovereign over the forces of nature, including rain, thunder, and lightning. A selection from an ancient document highlights this aspect:

> Moreover, Baal will send abundance of his rain,
> Abundance of moisture and snow
> He will utter his voice in the clouds [thunder]
> (He will send) his flashing to the earth with lightning.

The power of Baal over his own domain failed but Yahweh demonstrated that he had authority in this area.

The location and context of this event also had significance. It was at or near the top of Mount Carmel. Such "high places" were the preference of the Baal cult as numerous references in the Old Testament indicate (cf. 1 Kings 14:23, et. al.). Thus, once more, Yahweh demonstrated his superiority by direct intrusion into Baal's turf. Here we have a similar situation as in Egypt where the ten plagues represented

Yahweh's action in spheres supposedly controlled by one or more of the Egyptian deities.

The Aftermath

As dramatic as this event was, and even though it was followed by a purge of the false prophets, including the death of Jezebel, the results were only temporary. If we look at the message of Hosea in the eighth century, some one hundred years later, we find implicit in his time the resurgence of Baalism in the northern kingdom where Elijah's victory occurred. This eventual outcome reminds us that "signs and wonders" may affect the mind for the moment but they are unlikely to have lasting effect apart from the transformation of the heart, a truth that both Jeremiah and Ezekiel came to see. This truth is the import of Abraham's words to the rich man concerning his brothers, "If they do not listen to Moses and the prophets, neither will they be convinced even if someone rises from the dead" (Luke 16:31).

As great as Elijah was, and as convincing as was Yahweh's demonstration of his sovereignty over imposters, the only effective remedy for the waywardness of the human heart awaited one who refused to call fire down from heaven upon others or call for myriads of angels to come to his own defense when opposed and threatened by evil powers. G. B. Caird makes the illuminating suggestion that Elijah was typical of the whole Old Testament attitude toward the enemies of God and of his people because the Old Testament offered life and blessing to the obedient, and atonement to those who sinned in ignorance and error; but to those who willfully opposed God it offered only God's curse. Now, however, the Law of Moses and the way of Elijah were both being rendered obsolete by the determination of Jesus to follow the way of the Cross and by his redemptive suffering to reveal God's way of dealing with sin.

Demonstrating the Truth of the Christian Faith?

Throughout Christian history there have been those who have sought ways to "prove" the validity of faith in God and the truth of the Christian faith--and thereby "coerce" faith. This effort was usually made by philosophical argument. Simple believers never needed such underpinning to their faith and unbelieving philosophers were seldom, if ever, convinced.

The high point of efforts to prove rationally the existence of God occurred in the eighteenth century Enlightenment when human reason was elevated to the role of primacy over faith. Although living in the eighteenth century, John Wesley questioned the adequacy of such arguments. He explicitly denied that reason alone can conclusively prove this—or any other—theological claim. Wesley and his followers believed that the surest way to lead persons to evangelical faith was by a living out the principles of the Bible in character and life. Virtually all main line Christian thinkers today agree with this conclusion.

Nonetheless, there continues to be many popular attempts to convince and even convert unbelievers by rational argument based on the concept of reason inherited from the Enlightenment. These do not necessarily take the form of seeking to prove the existence of God, but usually more generally the truth of the Christian faith. They all attempt to argue on the basis of objective evidence from outside the faith itself, offering "evidence that demands a verdict." My college theology professor's implication was doubtless right when he would quote Psalm 19:1—"The heavens are telling the glory of God; and the firmament proclaims his handiwork"-- and quickly ask the question, "to whom?"

Since the nineteenth century, extreme Fundamentalists have attempted to "prove" the validity of the faith by appealing to the "inerrancy of Scripture." Since the existing manuscripts of the biblical documents clearly have discrepancies, people who advance this argument tend to appeal to the "original autographs" as being inerrant. Since none of these originals exists, this appeal is logically a case of begging the question. Finally, it is to be seriously questioned whether many, if any, persons have been converted to the Christian faith merely by being intellectually convinced of its truth by reason alone. Classical Christian faith, by contrast, affirms the authority of scripture on the testimony of the Holy Spirit not on the form of the text itself. It is of great interest that if the original autographs were of such critical importance why did God not preserve them. Instead, he has made good use of less than errorless copies. Evidently, it is the *message* of truth they convey energized by the Spirit that is significant.

The problem with all attempts at coercive proof is that they function within the worldview of eighteenth-century rationalism informed by the methods of natural science and mathematics. But some of the most important questions for human existence do not submit to scientific methods. Can a scientific analysis, for instance, assure me that my spouse loves me? Can science alone tell me that the Mona Lisa is a beautiful painting? Obviously, there is another dimension of knowing other than mere rationalism.

The question is how does one come to faith in and acceptance of God's saving love? The Wesleyan answer is not by coercive intellectual argument, or by "signs and wonders," but by the activity of "prevenient" grace. That is, God grants unmerited grace to us sinners while we are yet blind sinners. This grace enables us to be able at least to recognize spiritual reality, be convinced of our sin, and reach out in faith to the God who has reached out to us.

REFLECTIONS

While reflecting on Elijah's contest on Mt. Carmel, my mind returned to a scene from the past. In those early days, the holiness people would gather around a seeker for entire sanctification at the altar to pray them through. When the seeker "struck fire," often the folk would break out in singing, "I never shall forget how the fire fell, when the Lord sanctified me." Such scenes are rare these days, if not totally absent. However, it occurred to me that there was something significant in the analogy between God's answer to Elijah's prayer by fire from heaven and the concept of the fire of God falling on the seeker. It is certainly not the case that we can legitimately interpret the Old Testament story as an allegory teaching a specific New Testament experience. The relation lies elsewhere.

The fire that fell on Carmel was a vindication of the sovereignty of God. Its purpose was to convince the skeptics and those who "halted between two opinions" (1 Kings 18:21) that Yahweh alone should be the God of Israel. It was a powerful apologetic that, as we saw, temporarily convinced the people. It is highly unlikely that miraculous events that ostensibly occur today will convince a skeptic. We have become so informed by the scientific mentality that alternate explanations can easily be given. Intellectual arguments likewise convince those already convinced.

By contrast, if there is an authentic experience of entire sanctification--which I do not doubt--it too becomes a powerful apologetic for the power of God. The tragedy is that so often an emotional experience at an altar did not result in a radically transformed life. Richard S. Taylor suggested one reason for the "death of the holiness movement" to be the "shabby demonstration of holiness on the part of so many of its professors."[23] But this may have been the consequence of a faulty understanding of what entire sanctification is about. If this "experience" is viewed as a total commitment to the pursuit of Christlikeness, it entails a consistently ethical lifestyle. In fact, Jesus himself prayed for the sanctification of his follows in order that "the world may believe that you have sent me" (John 17:21).

One of my friends who was doing graduate study under a "church growth" guru told how at the close of the class, after having shared all the so-called principles of church growth, the teacher said, "But if you really want to grow a church, get into signs and wonders" and promptly marched out of the room. It may be the case that by that method you can grow a church but not the Kingdom of God. The most powerful argument for the Kingdom is the transformed lives of disciples.

Questions to Think About

1. Have you ever attempted to argue someone to faith? Did it work?
2. Are "signs and wonders" effective means of evangelizing persons not otherwise inclined to believe?
3. In this day when most people do not have a "Christian memory," how should we attempt to bring them to salvation?
4. How would you account for the near demise of "revivals" as a popular means of evangelism?
5. How important is a consistent Christian lifestyle as an "apologetic" for the faith?

---

[23]Richard S. Taylor, "Why the Holiness Movement Died," *God's Revivalist*, vol. 111, No. 2, March, 1999, 7-27.

Chapter Seven

MOUNTAIN OF EZEKIEL'S VISION

Revelation of the End of Exile and True Restoration

In the twenty-fifth year of our exile, at the beginning of the year, on the tenth day of the month, in the fourteenth year after the city was struck down, on that very day, the hand of the Lord was upon me, and he brought me there. He brought me, in visions of God, to the land of Israel, and set me down upon **a very high mountain** on which was a structure like a city to the south (Ezek. 40:1-2).

Ezekiel had been deported to Babylon from Jerusalem in 597 B.C. during the first invasion of Judah by Nebuchadnezzar. While there he lived among the exiles. His prophesying was primarily directed toward these exiles. His call to be a prophet occurred with a dramatic vision of the glory of God (Ezek. 1:1- 28), a vision that was the unifying theme of his entire ministry.

Ezekiel had been trained to be a priest and this gave shape to his theological understanding. This means that his perspective was informed by the holiness of God. It likewise **gave** him a special interest in the Jerusalem Temple that deeply influenced his visions and his prophetic utterances. Although some 550 miles away, the Lord gave him numerous visions of the conditions in Jerusalem, all related either directly or indirectly to the desecration of the holiness of the Temple.

The prophet's focus on the holiness of God influenced his interpretation of sin. The failure of Israel to maintain a life of integrity profaned God's holy name and brought dishonor to it. Repeatedly, Ezekiel emphasizes this theme: "As for you, O house of Israel, thus says the Lord: Go serve your idols, everyone of you now and hereafter, if you will not listen to me; but my holy name you shall no more profane with your gifts and your idols" (Ezek. 20:39). He recognized that their sins would result in the Lord expelling them from the land. However, this outcome of their sin was also a way of dishonoring God because the peoples of other nations would draw the conclusion that Israel's "god" was unable to protect and preserve his supposed people, not knowing that God was the cause of their defeat: "But when they came to the nations, wherever they came, they profaned my holy name, in that it was said of them 'These are the people of the Lord, and yet they had to go out of his land' " (Ezek. 36:20).

Central to Ezekiel's recognition of the incompatibility of the holy God and Israel's violation of its covenant commitment was the departure of God's glory from the Jerusalem Temple (Ezek. 9—11). As Ezekiel the priest was so well aware, the Temple was to be the center and symbol of holiness and moral purity. Any failure to maintain moral and spiritual purity would defile the sanctuary. Ezekiel is transported in one of his visions from Babylon to Jerusalem where he sees behavior that is defiling the Temple: "Then God said to me, 'O mortal, lift up your eyes now in the direction of the north.' So I lifted up my eyes toward the north, and there, north of the altar gate in the entrance, was this image of jealousy. He said to me, 'Mortal, do you see what they are doing, the great abominations that the house of Israel are committing here, to drive me far from my sanctuary? Yet you will see still greater abominations' " (Ezek. 8:5-6).

When the armies of Nebuchadnezzer ultimately destroyed Jerusalem and its beloved Temple in Ezekiel's absence, God gave the prophet a vision of its fall on the day it happened. Some time later a messenger came from the city to bring the sad word. This knowledge of the event before the news arrived was given to validate Ezekiel as a prophet so that the dispirited captives would have confidence in the message that he was now going to share with them. The destruction of Jerusalem was the turning point in his ministry (Ezek. 33:21). From this point on he became a pastor to the exiles.

The central section of the book of Ezekiel (chaps. 25-32) consists of prophecies against foreign nations. The purpose of this section is to assure Judah that those external obstacles to their existence as God's people in the Promised Land will be removed. With the external hindrances out of the way, the Lord then promised to deal with the internal problem. He expressed this hope in priestly language. Like Jeremiah, Ezekiel recognized that the basic problem of the "old Israel" was the lack of an explicit provision for an inner change. This message foreshadowed the later coming of the new covenant expressed in distinctly priestly language: "I will sprinkle clean water upon you, and you shall be clean from all your uncleannesses, and from all your idols I will cleanse you. A new heart I will give you, and a new spirit I will put within you; and I will remove from your body the heart of stone and give you a heart of flesh. I will put my spirit within you, and make you follow my statutes and be careful to observe my ordinances. Then you shall live in the land that I gave to your ancestors; and you shall be my people, and I will be your God" (Ezek. 36:25-28).

Bridge Between the Testaments

With the external hindrances out of the way the door was now opened for Ezekiel's visions of the future. These final visions justify designating the book of Ezekiel as the "bridge between the Testaments." Although the geographical exile came to an end under Cyrus the Persian, Ezekiel's vision never materialized. The events that followed showed no evidence of the glory he had predicted. In fact, it was a shabby situation. But if one will "cross the bridge" into the New Testament, we can find an amazing fulfillment of the vision as a consequence of the Christ event, although transposed into a new key.

In chapter 36 the Lord promises both a restored people and a restored land. The people will be restored to the homeland (36:1-5) and to each other. One of Ezekiel's most inspiring visions, easily interpreted, is the analogy of the two sticks (37:15-28). He is told to write the name of Judah on one and the name of Israel on the other and then place them in his hand in such a way that the two appear to be one. "Then says the Lord God,'Behold, I will take the people of Israel from the nations among which they have gone and will gather them from all sides, and bring them to their own land and I will make them one nation in the land, upon the mountains of Israel, and one king shall be king over them all; and they shall be no longer two nations, and no longer divided into two kingdoms'."

The northern kingdom of Israel had been virtually eliminated in 722 B.C. at the hands of the Assyrians, and Judah was soon to be no longer a nation. They would once again be in exile. But God's intention was for all of his people to dwell together in peace and unity. Thus, in Ezekiel's vision of the end of exile, the theological triangle of Yahweh, people, and land which summed up the covenant would be resestablished.

A New Temple

In the final recorded vision of his ministry, the prophet Ezekiel is carried up into a "high mountain" where he was given a detailed architectural picture of the building that would house the glory or presence of God when it returns. One writer characterized the major part of this vision as challenging any other section of the Old Testament for dull, boring, and apparently irrelevant reading for the modern student. Scholars have attempted to allegorize it, spiritualize it, or otherwise squeeze some meaningful juice out of it, but to little avail. No doubt it was exciting to the young priest, but pointless to Christian readers. Or is it?

Just as Moses on Mount Sinai was given the pattern for the tabernacle, now the prophet is provided a "blueprint" for the new Temple on "a high mountain." Blueprint might not be the right model to use since it appears to be three dimensional at points. He is led on a tour of the Temple that begins and ends at the eastern gate.

Consistent with Ezekiel's priestly worldview, the entire structure of the new Temple was designed with numerical symmetries and geometric designs to convey to the mind the impression of orderliness. Every society has a worldview that involves some classification system that orders what is thought of as "purity" in contrast to "pollution." The worldview of the priestly writing, including Ezekiel's, revolves around the ritual of the sanctuary and is dominated by a conception of *order* that extends through the cosmos, the sanctuary, and human society.[24]

The operative word in this understanding is "order." Holiness involves keeping faith with the categories of creation. In Ezekiel's case, the carefully ordered construction of the Temple is designed to represent a holy "space." As one moves through the various courts, the closer one gets to the Holy of Holies the more intense is the sense of holiness. Each court is elevated above the previous one, again indicating an increasing "grade" of holiness (cf. 40:6, 22, and 26). Outside the walls were the common realities of life. Beyond the land itself lay the unclean world of the Gentile nations. Inside the walls, however, was the sphere of God's presence.

The goal of the entire operation may be briefly described as the restoration of a divinely ordained cosmic order, which had been disturbed by sin. As magnificent as this Temple may have been, it stands empty and unused until in 43:1-5 it is energized by Yahweh's glory returning to take up permanent residence. This limitation echoes the familiar vision of the valley of dry bones (Ezek. 37) in which the

---

[24]Mary Douglas, *Purity and Danger* (London: Routledge, 1992). She insists that "the only way in which pollution ideas make sense is in reference to a total structure of thought whose key-stone, boundaries, margins and internal lines are held in relation by rituals of separation", 41. The key-stone to which she refers is "holiness," both God's and human.

restored nation of Israel was but an army of corpses until the Spirit of God gave life and vitality.

This final vision has three themes woven throughout. The first is the Temple, at which we have looked. The second is the sacrificial system along with an organized priesthood to administer it, and the third is the distribution of the land. As detailed in Leviticus, the sacrificial system had for its purpose the maintaining of the people's relation to God. Before the ongoing sacrificial rituals could begin, the altar upon which the sacrificial victims were to be slain had to be purified. Although a new altar was built, because of its continuity with earlier altars that had been profaned, an initial cleansing was necessary (43:18-27). This action suggests the preparation for a fresh start of worship in Israel parallel to the action of Moses in purifying and consecrating the original altar (Ex. 28:36f).

Following this initial week of ritual consecration, the regular pattern of sacrifices could begin, summarized in the phrase "your burnt offerings and fellowship offerings" (43:27). It is of great significance that these two offerings symbolized the vertical and the horizontal relationships involved in the covenant: the burnt offering being wholly given to God, and the fellowship offering being shared as a communal meal among the worshippers. Thus, the holiness of God that is a barrier to fellowship with sinful humanity is seen as the manifestation of grace providing the means of overcoming this barrier and establishing a restored relationship in both dimensions.

Of special importance is the "sin offering" that would be implicitly included in the general categories of sacrifices mentioned. The sin offering is designed for dealing with sin that has been committed ignorantly or unwillingly. Either one did something without realizing it was sinful or, knowing that it was sinful, did it despite intending not to. How "human" such things are! Likely, this "sacrifice" should be termed a purification offering dealing with ritual defilement. Contrary to popular interpretation, it has nothing to do with *establishing* a relation to God since it functions within the covenant relation already established. Rather, it concerns the maintaining of that covenantal relation previously established by grace.

In Ezekiel's vision, the priesthood is carefully organized to minister in the Temple and carry on the rituals involved in maintaining fellowship with God. Ezekiel's attention is then turned to the area outside the Temple walls. Since the land had been defiled by pre-exilic Israel, it too must be cleansed and the population resettled. In this new community of faith, tribal inequities (47:14) and the plight of the landless resident alien (47:21-23) are addressed. Thus, in this his final vision, Ezekiel describes a perfectly ordered Israelite society living in a perfectly ordered homeland under the leadership of a perfectly ordered priesthood serving in a perfectly ordered Temple. In a word, it would be a holy people living and worshipping and serving in a holy land.

Then, in the grand finale, Ezekiel's tour guide takes him back to the entrance of the Temple where he sees water flowing from under the south wall. It is forming a river that increases in depth as it proceeds southward toward the Dead Sea. At first it is ankle deep, then knee deep, and ultimately too deep for wading. Trees flourish along the bank. The river is alive with fish and the trees produce fruit in abundance because of the water that flows from the sanctuary. In a word, "everything will live where the river goes" (47:9).

Did Ezekiel's vision become reality? Not in the return from captivity when Cyrus gave the exiles permission to return home. Not under the Hasmoneans after they defeated the Seleucids and Judas Maccabeus cleansed the Temple from the "abomination of desolation." Not with the rebuilding of the Temple by Herod the Great. Rather, the reality stands as the hope of a visionary prophet who had transcended the negative and empirical evidence of his time to grasp the better world beyond. His hopeful vision reached out to the future and serves as the bridge to One who began his ministry with the announcement that the kingdom of heaven had finally drawn near, which meant that the exile really had come to an end and the full restoration had begun.

A Genuine End and New Beginning

Ezekiel's vision provides a wonderful reservoir of theological treasures. It is given to him in the context of exile in Babylon as a promise of hope that God will eventually bring the exile to an end. But when we look at the biblical story as it unfolds throughout the Old Testament, we can see it as an ongoing effort to escape from the exile that originated with the sin of the first pair and resulted in their expulsion from the Garden of Eden, foreshadowing Israel's expulsion from the land. When the Lord placed the flaming sword at the entrance to the Garden, it guaranteed that humanity would never be able to return on their own initiative. The flip side of this truth is that it highlighted the priority of grace in the restoration of humanity to their intended relation to God. The biblical story from beginning to end is a story of grace manifested by a seeking

God who desires to bring an end to evil and enable his creative intention to become a restored reality.

Ezekiel's vision for the end of exile incorporates a particular understanding of the "image of God." Out of the exegesis of the creation stories in Genesis 1 and 2 emerges a view of the image of God in which human persons were created. As we have noted more than once, it could be interpreted as a complex of relations that includes a relation to God, to others, and to the earth. A truly restored holiness will involve all three. The preceding analysis of Ezekiel's vision makes clear that these are the formative relationships that he sees involved in the restoration. Since "sanctification" is most comprehensively defined as the renewal of persons in the image of God, and the dominant concept of Ezekiel as a priest is holiness, the themes fit together like a hand in a glove.

In Second Temple Judaism, the period in which Jesus was born, there was the overwhelming sense that the exile had never ended. This perception helps us see the significance of the life and ministry of Jesus and the early church as the consummation of the centuries-old hope for the end of exile. As with other Old Testament expressions of hope for the future, we can see Ezekiel's vision finding the beginning of its fulfillment in the *Word become flesh* (Jn. 1:14). The result is that those who are identified with "the incarnate Word" have become the "temple of the Holy Spirit." Consequently, the temple filled with the glory of God is now to be understood as the church, the body of Christ energized by the Holy Spirit. The holiness of the church is guaranteed by the presence of the Spirit, and maintained by the sacrifice and priesthood of Christ, a truth at the heart of the Book of Hebrews.

Paul also envisions the church as the true temple and spells it out in the epistle to the Ephesians. In the process, he makes a major transformation in Ezekiel's vision. The Temple, for Ezekiel, reflected a kind of elitism represented by the elevation of each court several steps above the preceding one. When Paul is describing the church as the fulfillment of the Temple, all such distinctions are eliminated, especially the distinction between Jew and Gentile. He declares the Gentiles to be "no longer strangers and aliens, but you are citizens with the saints and also members of the household of God, built upon the foundation of the apostle and prophets, with Christ Jesus himself as the cornerstone. In him the whole structure is joined together and grows into a holy temple in the Lord" (Eph. 3:19-21).

The term translated "cornerstone" in Paul's description is a special architectural metaphor. In constructing a building, the builder first sets a "foundation corner" (the meaning of the term) that then becomes the point from which the building is both squared and leveled. Today one would use a transit to guarantee that the foundation is level, but it is the foundation corner that is the criterion. What the apostle is implying by this metaphor is that the entire temple of the church is level. All distinctions based on office, race, gender, nationality, etc., are done away with. We all stand on level ground at the foot of the cross.

One of the most exciting aspects of Ezekiel's vision is the river of life that flows from the Temple that has been filled with the glory of God. It creates a new channel through which it flows into the Dead Sea and transforms it into life, beauty, and fruitfulness. Several have demonstrated the significance of the difference between the Sea of Galilee and the Dead Sea for the life of both an individual and a corporate body. The beautiful, clear, and clean waters of the Sea of Galilee, teeming with fish, results from the fact that water flows in from the north and exits at the other end to form the beginning of the Jordan River. The Dead Sea, by contrast, has no outlet. Like the person who lives on the premise that they should be the center of the universe, the be all and end all with everything coming in and nothing going out, the result is stagnation, death, and desolation. But Ezekiel's vision is of a river that flows from the Spirit-filled Temple into this salty reservoir, transforming it into fresh water.

REFLECTIONS

Ezekiel's vision of the life-giving river is an exciting anticipation of a Holy Spirit-filled church. Congregations that are ingrown, concerned with their own sanctity and protecting it by building a figurative wall to the outside world, are normally devoid of much life. But those congregations that understand their holiness to be the dynamic of a fresh-water mission to the barren lands outside their doors are not afflicted by trivial disputes but enjoy the blessing of the glory of God in their midst.

John's Gospel gives us an insight into how this result comes to be. On the last day of the festival of Tabernacles Jesus declared, "Let anyone who is thirsty come to me, and let the one who believes in me drink. As the scripture has said, 'Out of the believer's heart shall flow rivers of living water' " (Jn. 7:37-38). If the stream of living water flows from Jesus, who is the embodiment of the true temple and promises to endow the believer with his own Spirit, the same stream of blessing, resulting in life, will flow from him through the believer. This outflow of the Spirit will bring abundant life to all who will "drink" of the life-giving water.

Ezekiel's description of the stream issuing from the Temple also gives us a remarkable analogy of the Spirit-filled life. One striking feature of the river is that it is constantly becoming deeper but without the inflow of tributaries. It is difficult to conceive of a life truly energized by the Spirit of God that remains sterile and stagnant. The work of the Spirit, as described by St. Paul, is to stimulate growth and vitality by both guiding and enabling the believer into an increasing conformity to the image of God as embodied in Jesus Christ. His classic summary of this truth is found in 2 Corinthians 3:18—"And all of us, with unveiled faces, seeing the glory of the Lord as though reflected in a mirror are being transformed into the same image from one degree of glory to another; *for this comes from the Lord, the Spirit.*"

The beauty and life-giving nature of the life indwelt by the Spirit can be seen by contrasting the healing powers that freely flowed from Jesus with the sterility of the legalism of the Pharisees who opposed him. We see little, if any, evidence of life as the result of their preoccupation with the traditions of the elders. Jesus, in love and compassion, was willing to violate all such restrictions to meet human need whenever and wherever it appeared. Likewise, his disciples, filled with the Spirit from the Pentecostal outpouring, spread healing in his name, a healing that grew ever deeper and soon began to cover the earth!

Life in the Spirit is an exhilarating challenge. When it is lived out in its fullness, it brings blessing not only to the recipient but to all that it touches. May God help all of us who profess the name of Christ to be open to the Spirit's work in our lives so that we can live fruitful lives and be a blessing to the world in which we live.

Questions to Think About
1. How does Ezekiel's vision of a new Temple illustrate the historically conditioned nature of revelation?
2. Do you see why Ezekiel can be thought of as a bridge between the Old and New Testaments?
3. How does the second half of Ezekiel's ministry reflect the faithfulness of God to the covenant?
4. What does the contrast between the Sea of Galilee and the Dead Sea suggest about the secret of a vibrant Christian life and a holy church?
5. What is meant by "we all stand on level ground in front of the cross"?

Chapter 8

The Stone That Became a Mountain

> "And in the days of these kings the God of heaven will set up a kingdom which shall never be destroyed; and the kingdom shall not be left to other people; it shall break in pieces and consume all these kingdoms, and it shall stand forever. Inasmuch as you saw that the stone was cut out of the MOUNTAIN without hands, and that it broke in pieces the iron, the bronze, the clay, the silver, and the gold—the great God has made known to the king what will come to pass after this. The dream is certain, and its interpretation is sure."
>
> --Daniel 2:44-45

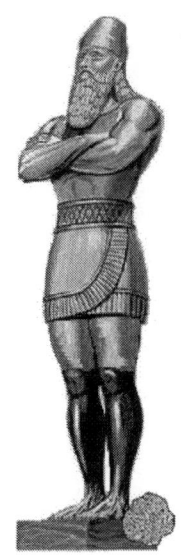

Revelation of Kingdoms and the Kingdom

The hope for the actualization of the Kingdom of God on earth in and through Israel suffered a devastating blow in 587 B.C. with the Babylonian Captivity. The symbol of the presence of God among his people, the Temple, was destroyed. The land where the Kingdom was to be located was desecrated and depleted of its population. Hope was on the verge of extinction and except for the latter ministry of Ezekiel (cc. 33-48) theoretically might have been abandoned.

Some 70 years later hope began to flower again as the Babylonians were defeated and Cyprus the Persian gave permission for the Jews to return to their homeland. Many returned with the expectation that their exile was coming to an end. Though a Temple was built it was a disappointment (Haggai 2:1-5). Disillusionment and cynicism took hold (Malachi 1:1-14). Most depressing was the fact that powerful empires still ruled the "chosen people." What was worse was that these rulers were pagans and a succession of such kingdoms deprived Israel of freedom thus it seemed impossible for the Kingdom to become a reality.

Under these circumstances the hope for the Kingdom began to take a particular form in the period between Malachi and Matthew. This time has traditionally been referred to as the "400 silent years" on the premise that the voice of prophecy had ceased. But these years were anything but silent. The shape in which the hope was given expression took the form of a special type of literature scholars have referred to as "apocalyptic," a word that means "revelation." This literature flourished during the time of Second Temple Judaism but of the numerous examples that appeared only one found its way into the Old Testament canon—the book of Daniel.[25]

This type of literature has preoccupied the attention of several scholars for years but has been particularly difficult to interpret and thus controversial. This makes it quite tenuous for a non-scholar (like me) to make definitive statements about its character. Nonetheless, the meaning of the passage upon which we are focusing is quite clear though expressed symbolically.

Apocalyptic is generally considered to be the response to situations of oppression such as would be the case with Israel's domination by pagan powers. As N.T. Wright says, "On all counts, apocalyptic can function, and we may suppose was intended to function, as the subversive literature of oppressed groups."[26] It is not escapist in nature since, contrary to much popular opinion, it does not envision the end of the space-time universe and is actually shaped by historical events. Rather, its symbolism, especially that of cosmic disturbance, is intended to invest historical events with theological significance. This characteristic is expressly illustrated in Isaiah 13, which refers to the fall

---

[25]There are several sections of apocalyptic in the prophetic literature. The Book of Revelation in the New Testament is generally considered to be an example of the apocalyptic type of literature but its theology is quite different. Instead of the conquest of evil making possible the establishment of the Kingdom of God occurring at the consummation of history, it sees that conquest having taken place at the mid-point of history in the death and resurrection of Jesus Christ. This is the import of the scene in Revelation 5 in which the only one able to open the 7-sealed book symbolizing the consummation is the "slain Lamb."

[26]*The New Testament and the People of God*, 288.

of Babylon. Verses 9-10 describe its collapse in terms of "apocalyptic" imagery: "Behold, the day of the Lord comes, cruel, with wrath and fierce anger, to make the earth a desolation and to destroy its sinners from it. For the stars of the heavens and their constellations will not give their light, the sun will be dark at its rising and the moon will not shed its light." Thus one of the obvious features of apocalyptic language is the use of symbols and images to represent nations and races. For example, Daniel 7:1-8 speaks of four great beasts that come up out of the sea: "Nobody imagines the writer to be suggesting that actual fabulous animals would be dragging themselves out of the Mediterranean and climbing up the escarpment, all wet and monstrous, to attack Jerusalem. The sea represents evil or chaos (see chapter 14), and the beasts represent kingdoms and/or kings as is explained in verse 17."[27]

Students of Daniel, since the 3rd century A.D., have been divided over the historical context out of which it arose. The traditional view is that it was composed in the seventh century while Daniel was a captive having been carried off to Babylon about 605 B.C. while Nebuchadnezzar was king. According to this theory the contents of the book with which we are concerned here are predictions of future events. And the widespread popular way of interpreting this position is to make those predictions refer to events yet future to our own time. In the light of this interpretation, John Bright's comments are pertinent:

> Daniel is the first, and one of the greatest, of the books in full apocalyptic style. But it is a sadly misunderstood book. It is not, as so many conceive it to be, a cryptic diagram of events yet to come so that, if one can only find the key, one may get from it a blueprint of the future. He who seeks to get this from Daniel has committed a major error of biblical interpretation: he has disregarded completely what the author of Daniel wished to say. The book of Daniel is, on the contrary, addressed to the author's own day, and is a mighty summons to courage and faith in the language of the Apocalypse.[28]

The other theory places its origin in the second century B.C. subsequent to or concurrent with the events that inform its contents.

---

[27]Ibid, 289.
[28]John Bright, *The Kingdom of God* (Nashville: Abingdon Press, 1953), 183.

Adherents of the first view argue that this theory is based on a denial of the possibility of predictive prophecy. The precision with which the events are depicted symbolically, if predicted rather than described, implies that history is determined since that is the only possibility of writing history in advance, even by omniscience. This, along with other strong reasons, is why I agree with most major scholars prefer the second theory.[29]

In either case the historical situation to which the book is addressing itself is the same. Although the stories in the first four chapters that have been so popular are about young men who lived in the Babylonian exile, it is generally agreed by the best scholars that in its present form the book belongs in the time of the persecution of the Jews by Antiochus Epiphanes. Antiochus' purpose was to force them to compromise their religious principles is vividly described symbolically.

With this background in mind we can now look at the narrative dealing with a vision or dream by Nebuchadnezzar that was interpreted by Daniel. The image in the dream represents the succession of kingdoms that have stood against Israel's freedom to be the Kingdom of God. The image in the form of a man was composed of diverse elements representing the characteristics of a series of kingdom. This vision correlates with Daniel's vision of four kingdoms in chapter 7 and is repeated using different imagery in chapter 8.

The different metals of which the statue is composed have declining value, from gold, to silver to bronze, and then all supported with a mixture of iron and clay. The relative value of these elements is reflected in a contemporary non-canonical document: "Say to [the earth], 'You produce gold and silver and bronze, and also iron, and lead and clay; but silver is more abundant then gold, and bronze than silver, and iron than bronze, and lead than iron, and clay then lead' Judge therefore which things are precious and desirable, those that are abundant or those that are rare?"[30]

In Nebuchadnezzar's dream, as Daniel explains, the head of gold is Nebuchadnezzar and/or the Babylonian empire. The chest and arms of silver represented the Medo-Persian Empire and the third represented the rule of the Greek kings following the conquest of Alexander the

---

[29] My first exposure to this way of understanding the message of the book of Daniel was in the late fifties through Bright's *Kingdom of God*. My first reaction was a question mark since it was so different from what I had been exposed to but it made so much sense that I found I could not disagree.

[30] 2 Esdras 7:55-57. Quoted in *The New Interpreter's Bible*, VII/54.

Great (this same sequence is graphically and precisely described in chapter 8). The full picture of the apocalyptic imagery in the book as a whole seems to make unequivocal that the fourth kingdom is that of Antiochus Epiphanes. But since these texts were so popular in the first century B.C. the rabbis identified it with Rome. This is why some very conservative interpreters today simply interpret it as Rome.[31]

The Kingdom of God is depicted as a stone (rock) carved out of a mountain "without hands." In contrast to empires originated and maintained by human hands thus making them unstable and ultimately destined for destruction, the Kingdom of God is an eternal kingdom that will endure because it is of divine origin. No matter how fiercely the pagan powers seek to destroy the Kingdom, they shall finally themselves be destroyed.

All this focuses on the hope for the end of exile. Fundamentally this involved the liberation from oppression, the restoration of the land and the proper rebuilding of the Temple. In a word, it would mean that God would be King of the whole world. This is clearly the import of the stone "filling the whole earth." This further implies, as N.T. Wright puts it, "The Kingdom of God, historically and theologically considered is a slogan whose basic meaning is the hope that Israel's god is going to rule Israel (and the whole world), and that Caesar, or Herod, or anyone else of that ilk, is not."[32]

In the first century the stone of Nebuchadnezzar's vision was understood by some as a prophecy of the messianic king. According to N. T. Wright some interpreters of that period made a linguistic connection between the stone (*eben*) and the son (*ben*). Since one of the tasks of the messiah was to fight the battle that would defeat the enemy and bring an end to the exile in that context it was natural that he would destroy the Roman Empire. The Jewish historian Josephus refers to Daniel in this way. This, of course, was a dangerous message, which partially explains why it is shrouded in the symbolism that is characteristic of apocalyptic. In this context, when John the Baptist and Jesus came announcing the Kingdom of God they were declaring a risky message, which doubtless explains why Jesus seemed to avoid messianic claims until near the end.

One need only read the rejoicing of Zechariah recorded in Luke 1:67-78 to recognize how pervasive this hope was: "Blessed be the Lord God of Israel, for he has visited and redeemed his people, and has raised

---

[31] For example see the introduction to Daniel in the Wesley Study Bible.
[32] *New Testament and the People of God*, 302.

up a horn of salvation for us in the house of his servant David, as he spoke by the mouth of his holy prophets from of old, that we should be saved from our enemies, and from the hand of all who hate us; to perform the mercy promised to our fathers, and to remember his holy covenant, the oath which he swore to our father Abraham, to grant us that we, being delivered from the hand of our enemies, might serve him without fear, in holiness and righteousness before him all the days of our life." But Jesus had a different battle in mind.

Josephus addressed the question of why the Jews pursued the course of violent revolt against Rome that led to the destruction of Jerusalem, the Temple and the nation by referring (somewhat ambiguously) to this passage in Daniel that "at that time one from their country would become ruler of the world."

That Jesus understood his ministry in terms of this Danielic vision is reflected in his reference in Luke 20:17-18 to Psalm 118:22—"The stone the builders rejected has become the cornerstone." What was so odd to many was that Jesus not only both taught and took the way of servanthood to accomplish the messianic victory. And he furthermore consistently warned Israel of the dire consequences of pursuing the victory over Rome using Rome's methods finally weeping over Jerusalem's failure to follow his way that would have been the way that made for peace. On more than one occasion Jesus tried to warn of the dire consequences of taking the course of violent revolution. In Luke 13 when some who told him about Pilate slaughtering people in the Temple during the sacrifices, he replied, "Do you think that these Galileans were worse sinners than all the other Galileans, because they suffered this? No; but unless you repent, you shall all likewise perish." We tend to interpret that as a warning of eternal punishment but in the larger historical setting he was warning about the destruction that would follow if they persisted in the course of violence they were pursuing. In context (see chapter 9) the concluding "wisdom" saying of the Sermon on the Mount is addressed to this issue: "Everyone then who hears these words of mine and does them will be like a wise man who built his house upon the rock; and the rain fell, and the floods came, and the winds blew and beat upon that house, but it did not fall, because it had been founded on the rock. Everyone who hears these words of mine and does not do them will be like a foolish man who built his house upon the sand, and the rain fell, and the floods came, and the winds blew and beat against that house, and it fell, and great was the fall of it." The house built on the sand represented building the Kingdom on military might whereas the house build on the "rock" stood for the way of "turning the other cheek" and "going the second mile." These words concerning the house on the sand came true in 70 A.D. when Jerusalem with its Temple were destroyed and Jesus' warnings were vindicated. Thus, when Matthew recorded Jesus giving this "sermon" early in his career he was seeking to reinforce the fact that the Kingdom of God was a different Kingdom from that of pagan powers but that in the final analysis it was this kind of kingdom that would ultimately prevail and the "meek shall inherit the earth." To this transformed Kingdom vision voiced on a mountain in Galilee we turn next.

REFLECTIONS

We are reminded that every nation and civilization of human origin and attempted perpetuation, like Nebuchadnezzar's statue, has "feet of clay" and will ultimately fail. One of the greatest philosophers of history, a British scholar by the name of Arnold Toynbee developed a wide-ranging theory of history that accentuated this point. In his work he traced the rise and fall of twenty-one civilizations, which he defined as the self-contained political and cultural product of a creative minority. However, when these elites cease to respond creatively to changing circumstances, and simply mimic an idealized past, they lose their legitimacy as elites. In a word, when the leaders of the civilization fail to creatively respond to the challenges it begins to decline and ultimately collapses by the weight of its own failures. A classic example of this pattern is reflected in the title of Edward Gibbon's famous work, *A History of the Decline and Fall of the Roman Empire.*

Toynbee was an immensely popular and influential historian in his time. The full twelve volume set has sold over seven thousand copies, and the abridgement over three hundred thousand. He was featured in *Time Magazine* and the BBC, and came as close to being a celebrity as a modern historian is likely to get. His reception among other historians was much cooler. He was frequently criticized for making sweeping generalizations, Civilization studies in general have been rejected for just this reason, Instead, they usually prefer to reject all such world-historical schemes, and work on tightly focused monographs that treat a manageable amount of evidence.[33]

---

[33]Philosophy of History Part XX: Arnold Toynbee and the Challenge of Civilization; December 3, 2015 by Daniel Halverson.

But the message of Nebuchadnezzar's dream is not a historical analysis of the inherent weakness and ultimate fall of empires but the fact that any secular entity that stands in the way of God's establishing His kingdom on earth will by that fact decree their own destiny. That is the import of Jesus' response to his critics as he explains the significance of the parable of the tenants (Matt. 21:33-41), obviously referring to the Jewish elite who have, in Toynbee's language failed to respond to the presence of Jesus as the one who is bringing to reality the Kingdom of God: "Anyone who falls on this stone will be broken to pieces; anyone on whom it falls will be crushed."

The picture of the stone smashing the pagan image in Daniel seems to suggest that the outcome will be the result of violence. And clearly, when those kingdoms fell they did so through violence. But when the Kingdom of God inaugurated by Jesus' broke the powers than held God's good creation in bondage it did so through a radical reorientation of the concept of power. It occurred through the power of love (see chapter 12). The practical implication of this transformation as it relates to the mission of the church is that the victory of God in Christ over the "principalities and powers" that occurred at the cross means that the mission of the church should likewise be "cross shaped."

This understanding of power is difficult to grasp since love appears to be the epitome of weakness and futile in confronting the powers of darkness. To do so is an act of faith that relies on the witness of the New Testament that in Jesus all principalities and powers have been taken captive (cf. Col. 2:15). After having completed a systematic theology in the Wesleyan theological tradition some years ago, I was invited to give a presentation at a conference to share what I might have learned about the mission of the church from my studies. Among a few others matters, I emphasized this point. A subsequent speaker from a non-Wesleyan tradition that emphasized "signs and wonders" responded to my proposal by saying "I resist the reduction of power to love." His concept of power was shaped by the world's view of power, rather than the gospel of Jesus Christ.

The picture we see in the dream of the Babylonian king, transformed through the Christ event, gives us confidence that, all appearances to the contrary, the Kingdom of God will someday fill the earth with the glory of God and the rulership of the King of kings.

Chapter Nine

SERMON ON THE MOUNT

Revelation of the Kingdom of God

When Jesus saw the crowds he went up the mountain; and after he sat down, his disciples came to him. Then he began to speak, and taught them, saying... (Matt. 5:1).

Photo by H. Ray Dunning

No doubt the most familiar collection of ethical teachings in the world is found in chapters 5-7 of the Gospel of Matthew. This section of the New Testament is commonly referred to as the "Sermon on the Mount." If this "sermon" was given by Jesus on one occasion, the precise location where it took place cannot be identified with absolute certainty. The traditional place is an elevated mound near the small city of Capernaum, a few hundred yards from the shore of the Sea of Galilee. An old church is found at this spot. It can be seen at a distance from the sea itself.

Biblical students have not found it easy to interpret the significance of this "sermon." This difficulty helps to explain the mass of books and articles seeking to do so. One source lists nearly 150 pages of bibliography on the Sermon. Views have ranged widely. On one extreme is the idea that the sermon is a series of attitudes, dispositions, and behaviors that are so demanding that their purpose is primarily to create a sense of failure. Another is the belief that it was intended only as an "interim ethic" on the assumption there would be only a brief interval between Jesus' departure and His return. Some have seen it as a description of the ethical life that awaits the enigmatic "millennium" referred to in Revelation 20. While it would be presumptuous to offer a "final" interpretation, I will offer suggestions gleaned in part from what I judge the best of contemporary interpretations.

Too many popular interpretations pay little attention to the sermon's context in Matthew or in the larger ministry of Jesus. They tend to treat it as an abstract body of ethical teachings. Thus taking it out of context helps contribute to the wide diversity of interpretations since it leaves it as "free-floating." So, my first proposal is that chapters 5-7 of Matthew must be interpreted in the context of the whole of Matthew's Gospel. Matthew, like the other three gospel writers, shaped his presentation of the life and teaching of Jesus in order to emphasize the theological perspective he was seeking to present. This observation raises the question of Matthew's perspective.

I am assuming what I judge to be somewhat of a current consensus, namely that Matthew writes as a pastor/teacher in his church, with an eye to the relevance of his material to the life and thinking of a typical first-century congregation. In this light it seems that one of the issues of such a congregation would be the relation of the church (Matthew is the only one of the Synoptic gospels to use the word) to Israel. Matthew is addressing both continuity and discontinuity, often in terms of contrast and "fulfillment." His assumption is the same as the rest of the New Testament, namely that the church is the heir of Israel. This relationship implies that the church is "the new Israel," as both Paul and Peter explicitly teach. We explore the implications of this assumption in the next section.

Gospel of the Kingdom of God

The first obvious objective of Matthew's Gospel is to present the "gospel of the kingdom." Jesus began his ministry with the same announcement as John the Baptist: "Repent, for the kingdom of heaven has come near" (Matt. 3:17). This objective suggests that Matthew placed the sermon early in Jesus' public ministry as an indication that these "ethical" teachings have an essential relation to the kingdom that is "at hand." When we take account of the various passages in the gospel that indicate Jesus primary mission to be to Israel (Matt. 10:5; 15:24), N. T. Wright's judgment is sound that this sermon is a challenge to Israel to *be* Israel, or put differently, it describes a new way of being Israel in contrast to the prevailing view of contemporary Judaism.

This conclusion is certainly implied by Matthew 5:20: "For I tell you, unless your righteousness exceeds that of the scribes and Pharisees, you will never enter the kingdom of heaven." This statement implies that Matthew's primary purpose is to contrast the prevailing Jewish concept of the kingdom of God with the nature of the kingdom that he came to inaugurate, or to contrast the "old Israel" with "new Israel."

If one compares the qualities that characterize kingdom people as described in the "beatitudes" with the expectation of the kingdom longed for by most Jews in the Second Temple period, we certainly find a sharp contrast. At least a majority of the Jews believed that the kingdom could only come when Rome was overthrown by force. This belief gave rise to a number of revolutionary uprisings.

Many Jews, including some of Jesus' own disciples, were ready and even eager to take up arms to help bring in the kingdom. Not only did Jesus warn that this approach was the surest route to destruction, but he made the contrary claim that it will be "the meek [who] shall inherit the earth," that is, see the fulfillment of God's promise to Abraham to possess and rule the earth. In this emphasis, Jesus appropriated an important resource from the Old Testament, Psalm 37:11: "But the meek shall inherit the land, and delight themselves in abundant prosperity." It is significant that Jesus expands the territorial boundaries of the "inheritance" to include the whole earth. This expansion was the original implication of the Abrahamic covenant and incidentally questions the widespread preoccupation of many modern evangelicals with a small strip of land in the Middle East.

The fact that the "beatitudes" (which may be viewed as the theological foundation of the sermon) are immediately followed by "you are the salt of the earth" and "you are the light of the world" is a further indication of their Israel-oriented significance. Israel, as the descendents of Abraham, was chosen, not for an exclusive relation to Yahweh, but to be the light of the world. Unfortunately, instead of functioning in this way, Israel had sought to restrict the light to themselves, deliberately leaving the Gentile world in darkness. Now Messiah Jesus was calling them to their original mission. In doing so, he reveals the nature of the kingdom of God that he is inaugurating.

The beatitudes depict Jesus Messiah as the fulfillment of the Old Testament promise of the one bringing about the age of salvation. In fact, the series of "antitheses" in 5:21-48 function loosely as an application and exegesis of the beatitudes themselves, making this whole section of Matthew an intensification of the Torah quite unlike that of the Pharisees whose emphasis was external and legalistic. Thus, we can conclude that the beatitudes may be read as an appeal to Jesus' hearers to discover their true vocation as the eschatological people of YHWH, and to do so by following the way of being Israel he was marking out for them, rather than the way of other would-be leaders of the time.

Many commentators notice that the summary statements of 4:23 and 9:35 form literary bookends for chapters 5-9. In these two nearly identical verses Matthew summarizes Jesus'' ministry as involving two aspects: 1) teaching and proclaiming the "gospel of the kingdom" and (2) healing people of their sicknesses. The Sermon on the Mount then presents an extended commentary on the first part of Jesus' ministry—his proclamation—while the following narrative (cc.8-9) presents an extended commentary on the second aspect of his ministry—his acts of healing. The "preaching" of Jesus is the *explicit* announcement of the presence of the kingdom whereas the healing ministry is an *implicit* announcement of the same. This latter is implied by Matthew 12:28: "If it is by the Spirit of God that I cast out demons, then the kingdom of God has come to you" In a word, the Sermon on the Mount is throughout a revelation of the nature of the kingdom of heaven.

Jesus, the New Moses

Matthew 1-3 seems to be shaped by the author to reflect the events of the Exodus from Egypt. It implies that the events of Jesus' life prior to the beginning of his ministry are comparable to the events of the Exodus: Pharaoh's "slaughter of the infants" parallels Herod's "slaughter of the innocents;" the passing through the waters of the Red Sea parallels Jesus' baptism; Israel's temptations in the wilderness parallel Jesus' temptation in the desert. And the temptations themselves are similar, being the temptations of hunger (Ex. 16:2-8), idolatry (Ex. 32:1-9), and testing God (Ex. 17:1-7). The difference is that Israel failed but Jesus triumphed, showing him to be the true "Son of God." The implication is that Jesus' ministry is bringing into being the long-anticipated "new exodus." Since the original exodus culminated at Mount Sinai with the establishing of the covenant and the giving of the law, Jesus' sermon given on a "mountain" is seen as the inauguration of the new covenant.

Many interpreters have focused on the mountain setting of the sermon, drawing a parallel with Mt. Sinai and representing Jesus as a "new Moses" giving a "new law." Viewing the sermon in this way is the source of the many disputes about how it is to be understood. By contrast to the idea of a new law, Matthew presents Jesus as fulfilling the Old Testament *prophetic* expectations by announcing and effecting the kingdom of heaven in history. As we have seen already from previous studies the prophets saw the great need of Israel and the "new covenant" they envisioned to be the gift of a "new heart" (Deut. 30:6-10; Jer. 31:33; 32:38-40; Ezk. 36:26-7). In other words, renewal of covenant and renewal of heart go together. Instead of a "new law," Jesus is inaugurating a "new relationship."

According to Jesus, entrance into the kingdom of heaven is not by any mechanical keeping a "law" but by following Jesus and thus entering into a *new relationship* that God is establishing with his own people through Jesus' ministry. The "ethics" that Jesus presents involves faithfully living out the fruit of this relationship—which necessarily includes both a proper relation to God and to each other. This interpretation avoids any legalistic interpretation of the sermon.

But what about the tension between the ideal and actual performance that has been present in virtually all discussions of the sermon? Since the entire New Testament recognizes that the kingdom of God was inaugurated by the work of Christ but awaits the eschaton for its consummation, that perspective is doubtless the best explanation of the tension. The sermon expresses both a "realized fulfillment" of the Old Testament hope and an anticipated perfect fulfillment in a future consummation. The disciple of Jesus is living in this "present evil age" but called to live a life corresponding with "the age to come" in which evil has been defeated through the person and ministry of Jesus Messiah.

The view that the Sermon on the Mount reflects a completely different starting point from "law" enables us to recognize more clearly how it is informed by the concept of the "image of God." As I have demonstrated several times in this study, the most adequate understanding of this biblical theme is in terms of a complex of relations (to God, others, possessions and oneself), all of which inform the Sermon on the Mount.

Living the New Law of Love

One of the most difficult aspects of Jesus message is found in Matthew 5:48—"Be perfect, therefore, as your heavenly Father is perfect." Interpreted in a legalistic way, this commandment clearly stands in tension with the prayer Jesus taught his disciples to pray, which includes a confession of sin and request for forgiveness. These difficult questions are mitigated when we recognize that Jesus is calling for a relationship with a special quality. The New Testament is clear that the Christian life should be marked by an increasing conformity to the image of God (2 Cor. 3:18). It is equally clear that this image is an ideal that we may more and more approximate but never fully actualize in this finite existence.

Living this kind of "perfected" life is not easy, but it becomes understandable. The Greek word translated "perfect" is *teleios* which is a goal-oriented term. When it is used in the Greek translation of the Old Testament (*Septuagint*) it describes one's relationship with God as a "whole-hearted allegiance to the Lord" and means "blameless," "righteous" (implying covenant faithfulness), "loyal," "clean," and "pure." Thus, the positive term *wholeness* best renders the force of *teleios* in such contexts. When placed in the setting of the Sermon on the Mount, the life to which Jesus calls his disciples is a life of the pursuit of "wholeness in Christ."

A New Relationship Not a New Law

The question faced by the average Christian is, "what do I do with these teachings?" Their rigor has been a major deterrent in attempting to understand how they are to be applied to the contemporary situation. It is, in part, the radical demands that have caused some interpreters to restrict application to either the apostles in the first century or to a future period of history. But, if inspired by God for us, the sermon must have relevance to contemporary Christian life. Even modern adherents of "Dispensationalism" who traditionally postponed its application to the Millennium have modified their earlier position and attempted to understand its relevance to what they term "the church age."

Let us note some principles unearthed above that will provide guidance for a practical application of the sermon's instruction. This analysis will be done in conversation with John Wesley's discourses on the sermon.

One of the first questions to settle concerns the audience. To whom are these teachings addressed? Again, some interpreters say that this sermon was directed to the first disciples only, while the crowds that followed them up the mountain were merely onlookers. John Wesley interprets Matthew 5:1 differently:

> Not the Apostles alone; if so, he had no need to have gone up into the mountain. A room in the house of Matthew, or any of his disciples, would have contained the Twelve. . . . But to put this out of all question, to make it undeniably plain that where it is said, "He opened his mouth and taught them," the word *them* includes all the multitudes who went up with him into the mountain.[34]

The sermon is for all of us who are willing to believe and dedicate our lives to the mission of God in this world.

At a more theological level, Wesley points out the significance of the order of the Beatitudes, which he identifies as "the sum of true religion." The first Beatitude signals the attitude requisite to entering the kingdom of heaven. To the question of the identity of the "poor in spirit," he answers: "Without question, the humble; they who know themselves; who are convinced of sin; those to whom God hath given that first repentance, which is previous to faith in Christ." However, this interpretation is not the only application since this attitude, along with "every other temper which is here mentioned, are at all times found, in a greater or less degree, in every real Christian." This dual reading means that the attitude of "poverty of spirit" is both the prerequisite for entering the kingdom and also for continuing growth in the kingdom since "the more we grow in grace, the more do we see of the desperate wickedness of our heart."[35]

When we come to the overtly ethical section of the sermon, the difficulties quickly appear. This section is where the history of interpretation reveals the greatest diversity. The clue to unraveling the issues appears to hang on whether we interpret the ethical injunctions as

---

[34] *Works of John Wesley*, 5:249.

[35] Ibid. 253, 257.

strict law in a courtroom sense or the way of living out *a new relationship*.

Many interpretations struggle with the identification of the ethical teachings of the sermon as *law*. The alternative we are suggesting is to view them as having to do with a complex of relations expressed by *love*. As Paul says, "love is the fulfilling of the law" (Rom. 13: 8-10). The commandment of love "cannot be realized as law, but only in faith in the love into which we are drawn and in which we are forgiven. We can love only 'through the Holy Spirit,' only when *God Himself* takes possession of us, by His love, and does *His* work through us."[36] What Jesus is doing, as he affirmed in Matthew 5:17-20, is not abolishing the law but emphasizing its *inner intention* and thus "fulfilling it."

There are other reasons, however, why one should be cautious about calling the Sermon on the Mount a "new law." A law applies universally and specifically, and the consequence of violating the law is always "guilt." The Sermon on the Mount goes beyond the kind of legislation that refers to overt actions and the related sanctions in order to deal with the relational matters of *attitude* and *disposition*. But no human court can prosecute a man for lust, or sentence a woman for failure to love. This limitation is clearly one reason why Jesus declares, "Except your righteousness exceeds that of the scribes and Pharisees, you will never enter the kingdom of heaven" (Matt. 5:20).

A further indicator of the problem of interpreting the Sermon on the Mount as law, even a new law, is reflected in the hyperbolic statements found in 5:29-30. Virtually no one holds that a person is to take these sayings in a literal sense. One early Christian did. Origen castrated himself but with maturity recognized the fallacy of such action. Are we to be literally tearing out eyes and cutting off hands?

How then are the ethical injunctions to be understood and appropriated? They indicate ways in which love may behave in certain circumstances. If we take Jesus' summation of the law seriously (Matt. 22:37-40), we learn that this understanding is what the various "commandments" of the Bible are, namely expositions of the one command to love. They are paradigms of love. The commandments are the God-given examples of what God's will and love mean in the concrete but always shifting situations of life. Brunner explains this interpretation well:

---

[36]Emil Brunner, *The Divine Imperative,* trans. Olive Wyon (Philadelphia: Westminster Press, 1957), 133.

None of the commandments in the Sermon on the Mount are to be understood as laws, so that those who hear them can go away feeling, "Now I know what I have to do!" If it were possible to read the Sermon on the Mount in this legalistic way the absolute and binding character of the Divine Command would be weakened, the sense of responsibility for decision would be broken, the electrical charge of the moral moment would be released, the act of decision would gain a false sense of security by having anticipated decision.[37]

This analysis suggests that the basic difficulty with the legalistic view of the use of the law is that it overlooks the diversity of moral situations and the complexity of the needs that must be considered in most situations. It assumes that to each class of moral situations there corresponds one moral rule which can be applied immediately, except in rare cases, to all situations of the class. In reality, it is seldom, if ever, that only one moral rule is relevant to a particular moral situation.

This view is close to what Brunner had in mind when he said, "God's command does not vary in *intention*, but it varies in *content*, according to the conditions with which it deals." Love is even more demanding than rigid laws—going beyond overt behavior to include attitudes and motivations. It also is more versatile and flexible because of its readiness to adapt to the messiness of real life.

Reflections

The interpretation that focuses on God's love in our renewed hearts sheds a brilliant light on the admonition found in Matthew 5:48—"Be perfect, therefore, as your heavenly Father is perfect." Clearly, this commandment does not call for a perfection of *performance*, otherwise the Lord's Prayer would be pointless in including the petition for

---

[37]Brunner, *Divine Imperative*, 135-6. Providing examples of how love may react in varied circumstances is referred to in ethical terminology as "casuistry." When these casuistic guidelines are treated as rigid law, as appears to have been the case with Pharisaic Judaism, it becomes oppressive. Brunner's discussion in extremely helpful here: "The error of casuistry does not lie in the fact that it indicates the infinite variety of forms which the Command of love may assume; its error consists in deducing particular laws from a universal law in ever greater and more scrupulous detail, thus it is wrong because it turns the Divine Command into a Law, and then inevitably into the sum-total of all laws" (134).

forgiveness.[38] But it does provide a meaningful return to John Wesley's teaching about Christian perfection, which he defined as "purity of intention." He repeatedly emphasized that this way of interpreting "perfection" does not guarantee perfection of performance, but it does demand a full yielding of the human will to God's will. It does demand being filled with the love of God and then living out that love—a virtual definition of Christian holiness.

Jesus' description of the Kingdom life in the Sermon on the Mount has the capacity to alternatively generate both hope and despair. It sets before us an enticing picture of a holy life. When we consider our frailties and shortcomings, we tend to despair of ever coming up to this exalted standard. But the emphasis of Jesus on the inner life in contrast to outer conformity to a legalistic standard implies what John Wesley called a "covered promise." Every challenge the Lord gives to us implicitly contains a commitment to provide the necessary resources to respond appropriately. I am not left to struggle to conform to this ethic in my own strength.

Oswald Chambers, in typical fashion, highlights this truth: "Who can stand in the Eternal Light of God and have nothing for God to censure? Only the Son of God, and Jesus Christ claims that by His Redemption He can put into any man His own disposition, and make him as unsullied and as simple as a child. The purity that God demands is impossible unless I can be remade from within, and that is what Jesus has attempted to do by His Redemption."

Paul's own testimony in Philippians 3:12-15 is an illuminating commentary on the Sermon on the Mount. In the space of four verses, he both denies and claims "perfection." Now Paul was no dummy. He knew what he was talking about. The perfection he denied was the full transformation of the Resurrection life. *The perfection he claimed was characterized by the single-minded pursuit of the perfection he denied.* This relation unravels the knotty issues involved in the claim of Wesleyan theology about the possibility of "entire sanctification" in this life. As Wesley loved to emphasize, it is a "single eye," a wholehearted pursuit rather than an attainment.

If we insensitively claim to have "perfectly" achieved conformity to the Sermon on the Mount, we run the risk of Phariseeism. If we completely despair of embodying its ideals in our life, we resign to

---

[38]Unfortunately, some holiness teachers and preachers of the 19th century understood perfection in this way and did, in fact, teach that entirely sanctified persons should not pray the Lord's Prayer, some evening denying that it was a Christian prayer.

mediocrity and possibly antinomianism. However, if we take it as the ideal that by God's grace we are pursuing with full intentionality, we will be living creatively in the "present age" by seeking to embody "the age to come."

Questions to Think About

1. How would you respond to persons who say that their religion was simply to live by the Ten Commandments and the Sermon on the Mount?

2. Is a full intention to live out the love of God what fulfills God's law—rather than a demand for the impossible, a perfect performance?

3. How does the New Testament teaching about the tension between the present reality of the Kingdom of God and its future consummation relate to the Sermon on the Mount?

4. Do you think the understanding of the Sermon on the Mount given here weakens or strengthens the call to Christian holiness?

5. Does the Sermon on the Mount teach a strictly individual faith performance—how I should act, or can it be applied also to the larger social problems of our day?

Chapter Ten

Mount of Olives

Revelation of the Vindication of Christ

"And as he sat on the Mount of Olives opposite the temple, Peter and James and John and Andrew asked him privately, 'Tell us, when will this be, and what will be the sign when these things are all to be accomplished?'"
Mark 13:3-4

Herod's Temple, as it was known in Jesus' day, must have been a magnificent structure. The contemporary Jewish historian Josephus describes it in glowing terms: "To approaching strangers it appeared from a distance like a snow-clad mountain; for all that was not overlaid with gold was of purest white." Even today, for one standing on the top of the Mount of Olives, the panorama of the holy city with the gleaming golden roof of the Dome of the Rock located on the ancient Temple site dominating the foreground, it is an impressive sight.

Model of Herod's Temple

As Jesus and his disciples were leaving the Temple precincts, they called the Master's attention to its grandeur (Mark 13:1). It is likely that they were stimulated to do so by the fact that the previous week Jesus had performed a symbolic act that implied the Temple's destruction and they were perplexed about its implications. They must have been shocked with Jesus cryptic reply that "not one stone will be left here upon another; all will be thrown down" (13:2b; par. Matt. 24-25; Luke 21).

The Olivet Discourse

Having arrived at the top of the Mount of Olives on their way to Bethany for the night, Jesus sat down and the disciples questioned him further about this prediction. His answer, with parallels in both Matthew and Luke, is his longest connected discourse recorded in Mark's Gospel and is commonly referred to as the Olivet Discourse. This chapter of Mark's gospel has been characterized as a chapter of great importance for the Christian believer and of great difficulty for the New Testament scholar. This latter fact partially explains why there is such a mass of scholarly, as well as popular, literature on this chapter and its parallels in Matthew and Luke. Virtually all scholarly proposals are presented quite tentatively. I have attempted to cut through much of the intricate, complex and technical discussions and suggested a relatively simple way of reading this discourse

The Olivet Discourse is the best-known statement of Jesus about what would follow his Resurrection and has been the fertile ground for speculations about the "second coming" and the end of the world. It has often been used to attempt to set up a timetable for these events as well as to identify the course of events leading up to them. However, making it into a blueprint for a future end of the world is taking this discourse out of the context and frame of reference of the Gospels. Actually the scripture does not ever envision the end of the space-time universe but its redemption (Isaiah 65:17; 2 Peter 3:13; Revelation 21:1).

The location for this discourse may not be accidental. Jesus seems to intend an allusion to Zechariah 14:4-5—"On that day his feet shall stand on the Mount of Olives, which lies before Jerusalem on the east; and the Mount of Olives shall be split in two from east to west by a very wide valley; so that one half of the Mount shall withdraw northward, and the other half southward. And you shall flee by the valley of the Lord's mountain, for the valley between the mountains shall reach to Azal; and you shall flee as you fled from the earthquake in the days of King Uzziah of Judah. Then the Lord my God will come, and all the holy ones with him." The context of this Old Testament passage is the coming of the divine kingdom (see Zech. (14:9—"And the Lord will become king over all the earth; and on that day the Lord will be one and his name one.") and the coming great battle of the nations against Jerusalem (see Zech. 14:1-3). This passage points to the Mount of Olives as the appropriate place from which to utter his last solemn oracle of judgment upon Jerusalem and his last solemn prediction of the vindication of himself and his followers.

The Context of the Discourse

The discourse must be understood in the context of the first century and the significance it holds in the ministry of Jesus, since the gospels were probably written either shortly before or following the fall of Jerusalem. It also has great significance for the experience of the early Christians to whom the gospels were addressed. No doubt the reason the words of Jesus survived in the memory of the Early Church was that they served a significant and useful function in the life of the Early Church.

Jesus' response to the disciples' questions is primarily a prediction of the events that will culminate with the destruction of Jerusalem and the Temple by the Romans in 70 A.D. The first Wesleyan commentator on scripture, Adam Clarke, recognized this fact and treated the text exclusively in these terms. In commenting on Matthew 24:1, Clarke says: "This chapter contains a prediction of the utter destruction of the city and Temple of Jerusalem, and the subversion of the whole political constitution of the Jews; and is one of the most valuable portions of the new covenant scriptures, with respect to the evidence which it furnishes of the *truth* of Christianity."[39]

Clarke did not explain the rationale for his claim that the destruction of the Temple was a *vindication* of the truth of the faith but the way he "exegetes" the text gives us a clue. Utilizing the descriptions of Josephus, he emphases the preciseness of the fulfillment of Jesus' prediction. For instance on the statement that "one stone shall not be left on another," he quotes the Jewish historian as saying: "Caesar gave orders that they should now *demolish the whole city and temple of Jerusalem,* . . except the three towers, . . and a part of the western wall, and these were spared; but for all the rest of the wall, it was laid so completely even with the ground, by those who *dug it up to the foundation* that there was left nothing to make those who came thither believe it had ever been inhabited." Thus, Clarke may be suggesting that such precise fulfillment of prophecy is the evidence of verification and is perhaps thinking about the words of Moses in Deuteronomy 18:15.

---

[39] Adam Clarke, *The New Testament of our Lord and Savior Jesus Christ* (Nashville: Abingdon, 1824).

Relation to the End of the Age

One of the major difficulties in interpreting this discourse is that the questions put to Jesus by the disciples apparently went beyond what he had indicated by his earlier pronouncement. In Mark 13:1-2 (Matt. 24:1-2; Luke 21:5-6) Jesus had unequivocally "predicted" the destruction of the Temple. Matthew's account makes it explicit that their question went beyond asking exclusively about the Temple and involved a query about the End of the Age. Although this language is not explicitly used in Mark, accord to C.E.B. Cranfield, the Greek word rendered "about to be accomplished" in 13:4 is an almost technical expression for the events of the End-time. Thus of the many thorny exegetical issues in Mark 13, the problem of the link between the destruction of the Temple and end of the age is surely the most perplexing.

The clue to adequately addressing this problem is attempting to interpret what the disciples meant by the "end of the age?" Although both popular and earlier academic interpreters took it to mean the "second coming" and the end of the "world," as soon as Christ said that *the Temple* would be destroyed, their thoughts naturally and immediately turned to *the end of the age*. However, it is important to note that, as good first-century Jews there was no reason whatever for them to be thinking about the end of the space-time universe. The "end of the age" about which they would be concerned was not the end of the space-time order, but the end of the "present evil age," and the introduction of the "age to come."

Another important fact that is no doubt shocking to popular piety is that in the context of Jesus' own ministry, we have few indications that He taught anything explicitly about His second coming prior to the Resurrection, as distinct from the coming of the Kingdom. His vocation was to be the divinely appointed agent to bring the history of Israel to its climax and inaugurate the Kingdom of God. The way in which he was living out that vocation was a mystery to his disciples. They were unable to take that on board and would have had little possibility of comprehending what lay beyond. The disciples were anticipating the coming of the Kingdom. Now they were confronted with the reality that the evidence that the appearance of the Kingdom was directly related to the destruction of the Temple, an event that would constitute both Jesus' vindication and ultimately theirs.

Fulfillment in the Near Future

There are clear indications in the Olivet discourse and elsewhere that the fulfillment of the predicted event(s) would occur within the lifetime of the immediate audience: Jesus said, "Truly I tell you, this generation will not pass away until all these things have taken place" (Mark 13:30). Mark 9:1 presents Jesus as saying, "Truly I say to you, there are some of those standing here who will certainly not taste death until they see the kingdom of God having come with power." As reported in Matthew 10:23, Jesus said, "Truly I say to you, you will not have gone through all the villages of Israel before the Son of Man comes," which doubtless may be related to the symbolic language used in Mark 13:26—"Then they will see the Son of Man coming in clouds with great power and glory." This description of the destruction of the city and Temple that is the vindication of Jesus' teaching about the Kingdom of God (see below) is obviously reminiscent of Daniel 7:13-14—"I saw one like a human being coming with the clouds of heaven. And he came to the Ancient One and was presented before him. To him was given dominion and glory and kingship, that all people, nations, and languages should serve him. His dominion is an everlasting dominion and shall not pass away, and his kingship is one that shall never be destroyed." The reference here is to a "son of man," surrounded and attacked by the monsters (pagan powers, notably the Seleucids under Antiochus Epiphanes), who is *vindicated*.

Does one take this language literally? Are we to assume that they will see Jesus riding by on a cloud? We must not be wooden literalists. Recent scholarship has come to understand that the purpose of such language was to invest historical events with theological or cosmic significance. It is actually a way of affirming, not denying; the vital importance of the present space-time order, by denying that evil has the last word in it.

All the evidence points to the fact that throughout Jesus' ministry, and particularly in the Olivet discourse, he was pointing to a decisive event that would occur in the near future. This event, as Luke makes clear with his straightforward historical reference to the approach of the Roman armies (Luke 21:20-24), is the consummation of the Jewish-Roman war in 70 A.D. I would suggest that this event did not bring in the Kingdom but was the event that vindicated Jesus' understanding of the Kingdom, both as to its nature and how it was to become a reality.

Relation of Historical and Eschatological

The basis for the preceding conclusion is the fact that Jesus clearly taught that the Kingdom was present in His own ministry and person. Demon exorcism and other miracles attested to that reality. However, the evidence also points to Jesus' understanding of a future inbreaking of the Kingdom. Jesus understood that the present reality of the Kingdom was not all the reality of the Kingdom. Its powerful, world-changing effect was yet to be seen. As a result, He taught that such a future expression of the Kingdom was on the way. His followers were to be prepared for its coming at any time. Thus the Kingdom is both present and future in the sense that the age to come has broken into the present although the present age has not come to an end. This fact would imply that there is both a historical and an eschatological dimension (having to do with the final consummation of history) of the Olivet discourse. The question is how are they related?

The suggestion of C. E. B. Cranfield seems to be the most balanced when he says that "In view of [the] evidence we would suggest that neither an exclusively historical nor an exclusively eschatological interpretation is satisfactory. Rather must we allow for a double reference, the historical and eschatological being mingled together."[40] The question is how they are "mingled together." The most unsatisfactory approach is to attempt to identify which verses refer to the historical and which to the eschatological.

Cranfield's proposal is that the "eschatological" is seen through the medium of the approaching crisis in history that occurred in 70 A.D., "the historical catastrophe being regarded as foreshadowing the final convulsion (without necessarily implying that there will not be other such crises before the End)." In a word, the direct and more-or-less literal fulfillment as described by Adam Clarke is historical in nature but as in other historical crises, the final crisis that will bring in the ultimate consummation of the Kingdom of God in its fullness is foreshadowed.

This interpretation is also how one should read the Book of Revelation. It had a definite message for those to whom it was written, and the meaning that they found should be the initial clue to its interpretation. The historical context is unequivocally the situation near the end of the first century when the Christians were faced with the possibility of persecution over the issue of emperor worship. The beast

---

[40]C. E. B. Cranfield, "Mark 13," *Scottish Journal of* Theology 6 (1953), 298.

that threatened them was Nero, whose full name (Neron Kezar) had the numerical value of 666. In other words, the issue of emperor worship (the historical) is in the foreground but the eschatological is in the background and should be interpreted in terms of the historical situation. This reference means that it is a misuse of the descriptions to attempt to identify a scheme of historical events by which one can predict, or even anticipate, the consummation of history. *The historical is transparent to the future but not an account of it as if by an eyewitness.*

The Fall of Jerusalem as Vindication of Jesus

What we are primarily exploring in this chapter are the theological implications of the historical dimension of the discourse and its fulfillment in 70 A.D. The hypothesis we are testing is that the national debacle served for both the ministry of Jesus and the Early Church as the vindication of Jesus' vocation to inaugurate the Kingdom of God.

The prevailing mood of Second Temple Judaism was marked by a deep concern to see the Kingdom of God become a reality in history. There were several different options on offer in the period for how it was to come about, all of which involved the throwing off the yoke of Roman dominance in order to realize the "end of exile." In contrast to Jesus' program as articulated in the Sermon on the Mount, the dominant method by which this hope was to be accomplished was to overthrow the Romans by Rome's methods.

Much of the mood of the period was influenced by the Maccabean crisis. Although there were significant diversities in the period, influenced by the successful Maccabean revolt against the pagan domination of Palestine in the mid-second century B.C. there was a dominant revolutionary mood. Most of the events in first century Palestine would have overtones of this war of liberation. It was kept alive by the annual celebration of Hanukah that memorialized Judas Maccabeus' cleansing of the Temple from the "abomination of desolation" resulting from Antiochus Epiphanes' sacrificing a pig on the Temple altar.

The climactic statement of the Sermon on the Mount concerning the two foundations graphically sets forth the contrasting outcomes of the two approaches. Like the consequences of building one's house on the sand, throughout his ministry Jesus consistently identified the tragic outcome of trying to establish God's Kingdom by violent revolution. The essence of his message is embodied in his word to Peter in Matthew

26:52—"all who take the sword will perish by the sword." His repeated warnings come to a head with the triumphal entry when he broke out in tears over the failure of Jerusalem to take his way with the inevitable consequence: "If you, even you, had only recognized on this day the things that make for peace! But now they are hidden from your eyes. Indeed, the days will come upon you, when your enemies will set up ramparts around you and surround you, and hem you in on every side. They will crush you to the ground, you and your children within you, and they will not leave within you one stone upon another; because you did not recognize the time of your visitation from God" (Luke 19:42-44).

G. B. Caird has given a meaningful summary of this whole scenario:

> Jesus believed that Israel was called by God to be the agent of his purpose, and that he himself had been sent to bring about that reformation without which Israel could not fulfill her national destiny. If the nation, so far from accepting that calling, rejected God's messenger and persecuted those who responded to his preaching, how could the assertion of God's sovereignty fail to include an open demonstration that Jesus was right and the nation was wrong? How could it fail to include the vindication of the persecuted and the cause they lived and died for?[41]

Reflections

Far too often, like the disciples, we may become so enamored with a traditional practice, institution or system that we ascribe to it eternal validity when God wants there to be a change. Apparently this attitude characterized the disciples regarding the Temple, an attitude that led them to challenge Jesus' declaration of its demise. One might presuppose that owing to the phenomenal costliness of the Temple, their eyes were so dazzled by the splendor, that they could scarcely entertain the idea that the kingdom of Christ would entail its destruction.

We find it easy to glibly criticize the reluctance and dullness of the disciples for their failure to understand what Jesus was about but experiencing a radical alteration in our own worldview may be just as

---

[41]G.B. Caird, *Jesus and the Jewish Nation* (London: Athlone Press, 1965). 20f.

traumatic. Accusing Israel for failing to recognize their Messiah when he appeared likewise does not consider the dramatic nature of how they would have had to abandon a long standing and deeply rooted tradition. In our case a similar reluctance, for less adequate theological reasons, causes us to resist changes in institutional practices, worship styles or non-essential practical behavior. While we should not change direction with every shift in the wind, we should have the courage to look carefully at the basis for our commitments and be open to follow truth when it is soundly based.

We may also find ourselves manifesting the same concern as the disciples in asking for a sign. The disciples want to be told what will be "the sign" by which they can recognize the approach of the End thus being relieved of having to watch. But instead of a single sign Jesus gives them a baffling multiplicity of signs. Actually Mark 13 is more of an exhortation than speculation about the end of the age. Instead of preoccupation with events that signal the end, it is characterized by words of exhortation such as "be aware' (v. 5); "do not be alarmed" (v. 7); "beware" (v. 9); "do not worry" (v. 11); "be alert" (v. 23); "keep awake" (v.35). In a word, the disciples must resist the temptation to speculate about end times or to be unduly alarmed even when this symbol of institutional religion collapses. The discourse is also peppered with the emphasis that "the End is not yet." Thus the primary agenda in the Olivet Discourse is not a description of future history, but an admonition to the disciples in their present circumstances to be alert in the face of threats, dangers, and uncertainties. This purpose is in contrast to those interpreters who have a tendency to make prophetic writings in the Bible into a prediction of a predetermined future. As a result they take the statements in the Olivet Discourse out of the context and frame of reference of first-century Christians and make them into a blueprint for a future end of the world.

Someone has said that "the only thing we learn from history is that we do not learn from history." This dictum is certainly true when it come to speculating about the future. Failure after failure does not deter pop prophecy buffs from seeking to identify what they think to be hidden clues that provide the information they need to set dates. One of the buzz-words of these approaches is "signs of the times." These are supposed to be indications that the end is near but this meaning is not what the one time the term is used in the New Testament means. In Matthew 16:3 Jesus says to his critics, "You know how to discern the appearance of the sky, but you cannot interpret the signs of the times."

This response refers to the way the appearance of the sky at sunrise and sunset predicts the weather. I learned this wisdom from my grandmother when I was a child and later used it to determine whether to plan a fishing trip. She taught me the formulas, "red in the morning, sailor take warning," and "red at night sailor's delight." Put differently, "evening red and morning gray sends the traveler on his way." It almost always worked, although it didn't guarantee that the fish would bite. The point Jesus was making was that the "signs of the times,"—his healings, his table fellowship, his teachings—were signs, not that the Kingdom was about to arrive but that it was already here. And his opponents with a totally different concept of the Kingdom were too blinded by their worldview to recognize them.

That there is to be a future appearance of the Crucified One in judgment and consummation is a fundamental truth of scripture and a fundamental affirmation of faith by the church, as is evidenced by the Apostle's Creed. But biblical prophecy speaking about this future event does not have for its purpose the satisfying our curiosity. It is instructive to see how the New Testament writers used this hope of the Advent. They never made it a subject for speculation; it was always a spur for Christian attitudes and Christian action.

Questions to Think About

1. What will be the likely aftermath of a failed prediction of the date of the Second Coming?

2. Explore the meaning of "cognitive dissonance" in relation to prophets who set dates that fail and then recalculate?

3. Are there phenomena today that can serve as vindication of the church's claims about Jesus?

4. Do you see a danger in insisting on a literal fulfillment of "apocalyptic" imagery?

Chapter Eleven

MOUNT TABOR

Revelation of the Glory of Christ

Six days later, Jesus took with him Peter and James and John and led them up a high mountain apart, by themselves. And he was transfigured before them; his clothes became dazzling white, such as no one on earth could bleach them. And there appeared to them Elijah with Moses, who were talking with Jesus. Then Peter said to Jesus, "Rabbi, it is good for us to be here; let us make three dwellings, one for you, one for Moses, and one for Elijah." He did not know what to say, for they were terrified. Then a cloud overshadowed them and from the cloud there came a voice, "This is my Son, the Beloved; listen to him!" Suddenly when they looked around they saw no one with them any more, but only Jesus" (Mark 9:2-8).

Mt. Tabor

Mount Tabor is the traditional site for the "transfiguration of Christ." Some have suggested that it was Mount Hermon but the Gospel writers do not identify the specific location, referring only to a "high mountain." The most important issue for our purposes is not the exact site but the revelational meaning of the event.

We need to examine this event very carefully since there may be no other incident recorded in the Gospels that has been interpreted in such a variety of ways. This diversity is why it has been characterized as at once the commentator's paradise and his despair. The Transfiguration has been referred to as the "Gospel in Microcosm" because it has a connection with Jesus' Baptism, Caesarea Philippi, Gethsemane, the Crucifixion, the Resurrection, the Ascension, and the Parousia.

A number of scholars have interpreted the Transfiguration as a "misplaced Resurrection appearance." However, if we accept the integrity of Scripture, we shall see it as a "red letter" event in the unfolding of Jesus' ministry. There are a number of similarities and differences among the three accounts of the transfiguration (Mk. 9:2-8; Matt. 17:1-8; Lk. 9:28-36). What is most important is the rich complexity of theological motifs to be found in the three accounts of the event. And these theological motifs appear to be all interrelated.

The Theological Significance

I suggest that the central theological significance of this amazing event is found in the fact that it is one instance of a pattern that is present in the synoptic accounts. There were four pivotal pairs of events in the ministry of Jesus, each pair signaling a significant moment in his life and each event interpreting the one with which it is paired. All point in the same direction. All four signal a major transformation in the nature of the Old Testament hope of a future Messiah and the Kingdom of God.

1. Baptism and Temptation. The first pair includes Jesus' baptism and his temptation in the wilderness. While several theological meanings may be derived from the baptism of Jesus by John in the Jordan River, the most revolutionary aspect comes to expression in the words from heaven: "This is my beloved Son, with whom I am well pleased" (Matt. 3:17). These words constitute an ordination formula that launches Jesus into the vocation that shaped his life throughout.

These words were a combination of inaugural statements from the Old Testament. The first phrase is taken from Psalm 2:7 used in the installation of a Judean king. Each king was inducted into office with the hope that he might become the "king like David" who would restore Israel to the glory she had enjoyed under the Davidic rule. In a word, it was the expression of what subsequent interpreters have called the Messianic hope.

The second phrase is taken from Isaiah 42:1 and was an ordination announcement referring to the servant of the Lord, a figure that appears throughout Isaiah 40-55. He is one whose mission is to suffer vicariously to bring about the redemption of mankind as most graphically pictured in Isaiah 53. The joining of these two visions is unique in that nowhere in previous expressions of hope for the future did any Jewish literature join them in one person. In fact, the dominant Messianic hope came to preclude suffering, except as it was inflicted on those who opposed the Messiah. Thus what we have in Jesus' baptism, interpreted by the words from heaven, is the introduction of the vocation of a "suffering Messiah," something totally unanticipated. The baptism of Jesus was a proleptic event, one that pre-enacted the cross.

Shortly after his baptism Jesus was "led up by the Spirit into the wilderness to be tempted by the devil" (Matt. 4:1). Once again, several theological and practical truths regarding the nature of temptation can be drawn from this experience, but its relation to the baptism is probably most significant. The three temptations were proposals to divert Jesus from his vocation of bringing about redemption through suffering. What was being suggested to him by the evil one were alternate ways of living out the messianic vocation.

The first temptation was to be an *economic* Messiah. The second was to be a *marvelous* Messiah, but Jesus consistently refused to put on a stunt show. The third was to be a *political* Messiah, but no earthly kingdom is or can be the kingdom of God. Evil men may in a measure be restrained by force, but their inner transformation cannot be coerced and that was the critical need of the human heart.

2. Mass Feeding and the Bread of Life. The second pair of events includes the feeding of the 5000 and the discourse on the Bread of Life (found only in John). The great significance of the miraculous feeding is suggested by the fact that it is the only miracle performed by Jesus reported by all four gospels. This event once again raised the issue of the nature of messiahship since the people took the event as a sign that Jesus was the long-awaited Messiah who would provide for their physical needs. As a result they sought to "take him by force" (Jn. 6:14). Since this understanding was a perversion of the vocation for which Jesus had been anointed at his baptism, he quickly absented himself from the situation.

Not to be deterred, the now expectant crowd tracked him down with the intent of declaring him as their "king." John alone tells us that in response he identified himself as the *bread from heaven* rather than a provider of physical bread and indicated that participation in him would have its high cost. With this recognition many of his disciples said: "This teaching is difficult, who can accept it?" and turned back from following him (Jn. 6:60-71).

This pair of events constitutes a major turning point in Jesus' ministry. He now focused his attention on preparing his disciples for the developments that he knew would be the outcome of his ministry. We come finally to the third pair of events, the confession of Peter at Caesarea Philippi and the Transfiguration itself.

3. *Peter's Confession and the Transfiguration.* Once again, as with the first two pairs of events, the issue involved the nature of messiahship. Now that his disciples had come to the conclusion that Jesus was the Christ (Messiah), they were confronted with a major worldview transformation.

Up to this point Jesus' teaching about his vocation had been veiled. Now, Matthew tells us, he begins to speak openly of it: "From that time on, Jesus began to show his disciples that he must go to Jerusalem and undergo great suffering at the hands of the elders and chief priests and scribes, and be killed, and on the third day be raised" (Matt. 16:21). Peter's response demonstrates how deeply rooted in the Jewish consciousness was the idea of a political and military messiah. He took it on himself to straighten out the Master's theology but Jesus recognized in his words the temptation in the wilderness. That is the point of his response, "get behind me Satan."

Matthew and Mark tell us that six days later Jesus took the three of his closest companions, Peter, James, and John, up a "high mountain" where the transfiguration of Jesus occurred. Luke says it was about eight days later. The one item that seems to carry the most central theological significance of the event on the mountain is the word spoken from the cloud--from God. This brief message is clearly intended to be reminiscent of the baptism of Jesus. The words are nearly identical. The new element is the phrase "listen to him." The "inner circle" of the disciples was being enjoined to pay attention to the transformed worldview to which they had been introduced at Caesarea Philippi.

What Jesus had explained to them as imminent was indeed God's plan for the messianic deliverance of Israel, and of the whole world. They should give heed to this transformation in how that plan was to be implemented. This new understanding is precisely how Peter later explained what had happened to them on the mountain: "For we did not follow cleverly devised myths when we made known to you the power and coming of our Lord Jesus Christ, but we had been eyewitnesses of his majesty. For he received honor and glory from God the Father when that voice was conveyed to him by the Majestic Glory, saying, 'This is my Son, my Beloved, with whom I am well pleased.' We ourselves heard this [same] voice come from heaven while we were with him on the holy mountain. So we have the prophetic message more fully confirmed" (2 Pet. 1:16-19a).

This emphasis is not to say that all the other aspects of the phenomenon of Jesus' transfiguration were merely window dressing. There were several other significant points that impinge on this central one. Like the baptism itself, the transfiguration is a "proleptic" experience—it prefigures and is an advance taste of the coming resurrected Christ. This relation probably explains the early interpretations of the event as a "misplaced resurrection appearance." It is here that the concept of "glory" is anticipated. "Glory" is generally the term drawn from the Old Testament to express that which people can apprehend of the presence of God on earth.

The reality of this dramatic unveiling is captured in Charles Wesley's Christmas hymn, "Hark! The Herald Angels Sing:"

> Veiled in flesh the Godhead see;
> Hail th' incarnate Deity,
> Pleased as man with men to dwell,
> Jesus our Immanuel!

Moses at Sinai and the Transfiguration

A further implication emerged from the remarkable parallel between Moses at Mount Sinai and the event of the transfiguration of Jesus. Note the similarity to Exodus 24:15-16: "Then Moses went up on the mountain, and the cloud covered the mountain. The glory of the Lord settled on Mount Sinai, and the cloud covered it for six days; on the seventh day he [God] called to Moses out of the cloud." Upon Moses descent from the mountain, his face shone with the glory of God. Luke, in his description of the transfiguration, noted that Jesus' face shone. We are doubtless intended to assume that this reference is a testimony to the fact that Jesus is the prophet like Moses of whom Moses himself said, "you shall heed such a prophet" (Deut. 18:15).

This parallel with Moses includes a most significant element reported only by Luke. He reports that Jesus, Moses, and Elijah spoke about Jesus' *exodos*. The Greek term has been variously translated into English as "death" or "departure," but the literal reading suggests a most important salvation-related truth. Just as Moses had been the agent through whom God had delivered Israel from the bondage of Egypt in the first exodus, so now the Son of God was in the process of enacting a "new exodus" from the "exile" of the captivity of sin.

Ever since the Babylonian captivity of 587 B.C., Israel had remained in exile. Although some had returned to the homeland under Cyrus the Persian, they were still under pagan rule and remained so, except for a brief period of independence under the Maccabean dynasty. All that time they longed for release, hoping once again to be a free people under God. They expressed this hope in terms of the great act of deliverance that had brought them into being as a nation in the first place. Once again, the prophets declared, God would act to overthrow pagan powers and liberate his people. Now in the transfiguration of Jesus, we learn, God is about to do just that, but in a fashion totally unanticipated by the prevailing hope. The triumph was to occur through submission and suffering, not through military might. Rome was to be overthrown without using Rome's military methods.

Moses and Elijah

There is a further question about the appearance of Moses and Elijah on the mount of transfiguration. What was its purpose? The popular interpretation is that they represent the law and the prophets who are witnesses to the validity of Jesus' transformation of the messianic hope. While this much is likely true, there appears to be a more significant implication, not simply from their appearance, but perhaps more importantly by their disappearance. It is true that both, in Jewish tradition, had experienced an "assumption," being transferred to the more excellent glory before physical death. But the theological meaning apparently arises from the fact that at Caesarea Philippi the disciples reported that the common people were identifying Jesus with "Moses or one of the prophets," and in Jewish tradition Elijah was the paradigmatic prophet who had special status with Israel.

We learn from the larger context that Elijah had already come in the person of John the Baptist. But is Jesus simply a "new Moses?" The fact that both Moses and Elijah faded away, leaving "Jesus only" (Mk. 9:8), tells us that those who represented the old order were passing away. That old order was now giving place to a fuller and more adequate revelation of God's character and purpose. For all the splendor of their achievement, they and the covenant within which they stood had failed." There is only One who now is the manifestation of the glory of God, and whose work will address the weakness of the Old Covenant. This emphasis is Paul's point in Romans 8:3—"For God has done what the law, weakened by the flesh, could not do: by sending his own Son in the likeness of sinful flesh, and to deal with sin, he condemned sin in the flesh..."

This point is reinforced by the proposal of Peter that they build three tabernacles (Mk. 9:5, KJV) and stay in this glorious spot on the mountain. The tabernacle and subsequently the Temple were central to the old order, the dwelling place of the glory or presence of God. Now, we are learning, we are to find the glory of God only in the person of Jesus Christ. And that glory, Paul reminds us in 2 Corinthians 3:18, becomes the pattern by which we are to order our lives. In fact, as G. B. Caird noted, the whole history of Christian ethics could be written as a commentary on the Transfiguration.

From the New Testament point of view, the fourth pair of events to which we referred earlier, came at the climax of Jesus' ministry. They are the *cross* and the *resurrection*. These two pivotal events are to be taken in combination as *the hinge of all salvation history*.

Reflections

Of all the mountains of divine revelation, the one that occurred on Mount Tabor most clearly connects to the subsequent experiences in the valley. Briefly put, the little group who had been present at the transfiguration descended from the heights to find an epileptic child, a frustrated parent, and a group of puzzled disciples. Although Jesus had earlier given them power to "cast out demons," their effort in this case was futile. Sounding a bit frustrated at the slowness of his disciples to grasp his teaching, Jesus casts out the demons. Then, in private, he responds to his disciples' question about their ineffectiveness.

Although all three of the Synoptic Gospels report the puzzlement of the disciples, each reports a different response by Jesus. According to Matthew, Jesus said, "because of your little faith" (17:29). Mark reports the brief reason being "this kind cannot be driven out by anything but prayer" (9:29). As a young preacher I was deeply influenced by G. Campbell Morgan's little classic on preaching. In working through it, I was somewhat shocked by his illustration of one preaching principle: "be sure your text is in the Bible." As an example, he referred to this passage in Mark and explained that the words in the King James Version, "and fasting," were not really in the text. At that time I knew nothing about textual criticism, but Morgan explained that these words were not in the best original manuscripts. My seminary New Testament professor, Ralph Earle, confirmed the same thing in his commentary on Mark. Though slightly different, the context of Mark involves Matthew's emphasis on the centrality of faith (9:23-24).

Evidently, we should understand that there is an intimate connection between prayer and faith. It is Luke who emphasizes that the transfiguration event itself occurred in the context of prayer (Lk. 9:18, 28), and so highlights the importance of this relationship. Prayer is to be a life of intimacy with God, not merely occasional times of speaking with God. It is a daily discipline, a constant reliance on God and his transforming power.

In Luke's account of the developments "in the valley," Jesus offers an enigmatic response to their amazement at his healing: "Let these words sink into your ears; for the Son of Man is to be delivered into the hands of men." As usual, they did not understand. Joel Green points out the significance of the obvious manifestation of majesty and glory that apparently lingered on his countenance from the mountain. That significance lies in connecting Jesus' identity with "the Son of Man is going to be betrayed into human hands." The almost immediate response of the disciples demonstrates a portrait of the bankruptcy of faith and perceptiveness. Deeply impressed with the "glory" pole of the paradox, they immediately began to debate among themselves as to who would be the greatest when the kingdom is established. They had yet to comprehend the radical transformation of the concept of power that was occurring with Jesus.

The transfiguration revelation was a pivotal moment in answering a question that had surfaced throughout Jesus' life. His actions engendered curiosity. His teaching created astonishment. The question that seemed to be on all minds was, "who is this man?" Even his own parents seemed a bit puzzled as a result of his response to their rebuke when they finally located him in the Temple (Lk. 2:50). His fellow citizens recognized him as Joseph's son but noticed that there was something different about him (Lk. 4:20). The custodians of religious tradition were both perplexed and incensed that he presumed to speak words of forgiveness. Who but God could do this? In desperation they even accused him of colluding with the devil. Even his own disciples were shocked by his calming the wind and the waves. Mark says, "They were filled with awe, and said to one another, 'who then is this that even the wind and sea obey him?'" (4:41)

This response is quite strange when we recall that they had seen Jesus heal the sick, cast out demons, and even raise the dead (Lk. 7:15). The answer to the true identity of Jesus is found in one of the most pervasive but little recognized themes in all of Scripture. It runs from Genesis 1:1 to Revelation 21:1. From the initial conquest of "the sea" (symbolic of chaos) there was a constant threat to the good creation, a force that only God could hold back. They were afraid of the sea, being "land-lubbers." Thus, it became natural to use this symbolism.[42] The point is that only God can still the sea (chaos).

Finally, at Caesarea Philippi Jesus takes a survey to see what conclusion has been reached about his true identity. He finds that his disciples had eventually drawn the right conclusion but still did not understand its implications. The disciples were being faced with one of the most difficult tasks any of us can face, changing our total way of looking at things. The transfiguration was a major blow to the disciples' old worldview and an opening of a new one for them. Our way of looking at and interpreting our world becomes deeply entrenched in our very personality, normally as a result of cultural environment. The result, when faced with an alternative world view, even with compelling evidence, is described in an old adage, "a man convinced against his will is of the same opinion still."

Their transformation did not occur suddenly or completely as a result of this revelation. In fact, it took a long time. I am reminded of my own struggle in breaking free from the view of eschatology to which I had been exposed all my early life in the church. It only took place in bits and pieces as I tried to make sense of certain passages of Scripture as a pastor seeking to lead the thinking of my people. All the preaching I had heard presented a definite pattern of end-time events that, among other things, had the church "raptured" out of the world, followed by a great tribulation. In trying to make sense of the book of Revelation, I finally came to see, I thought, that if I abandoned the idea of a "secret rapture" and left the church in the tribulation, the book would make sense. Of course, any biblically literate person will immediately recognize that this change was but a minor adjustment *within* the largely unchanged worldview.

It took me years to recognize the unbiblical presuppositions that informed that whole worldview sometimes known as Dispensationalism.

---

[42]For a full development of this theme, see Bernhard Anderson, *Creation and Chaos* (Philadelphia: Fortress Press, 1966); Norman Young, *Creator, Creation, and Faith (*Philadelphia: Westminster Press, 1976).

I managed (I think) to escape this set of misconceptions. How traumatic this transformation was became clear to me when I began teaching and students sometimes reacted almost violently to my exposing them to the fallacies of their end-times inheritance. Eventually, most of them felt liberated. In a similar way, the vision to which the disciples were exposed at the Caesarea Philippi examination, reinforced by the transfiguration, is far more significant than a revised eschatology. Although the transformation entailed great pain it resulted in a new worldview for them! A more profound understanding of who Jesus is and what he came to do may open a whole new world for us as well.

It is apparent that the nature of authentic discipleship is dependent on how we answer the question of who Jesus is, a crucial issue for all of us who would be his followers. We must come to see that he is more than the world's greatest teacher, though he was. We must come to see that he did more than offer us a new form of religious experience though he did that too. We must come to see that, through his death, resurrection, and glorification, he brought into existence a new order of being, a "new creation." We must learn to live in the light of this dramatic new reality. All this becomes brilliantly clear in the revelation of the worldview that took place on Mount Golgotha, to which we turn next.

Questions to Think About

1. How would you describe the relation between Jesus' humanity and his deity?
2. What is the proper Christian motive in aspiring to leadership in the church?
3. In what ways have you changed your mind on some really big issue? How difficult was it to do?
4. Are there ways in which we may compromise the centrality of Jesus Christ?

Chapter Twelve

MOUNT GOLGOTHA

Revelation of the Power of Love

"When they came to the place called the Skull, they crucified him there, along with the criminals—one on his right, the other on his left." (Luke 23:33, NIV)

Photo by H. Ray Dunning

In the mid 1970s I had the opportunity to join a group of pilgrims to Israel. At one point during the tour, we stood on a wooden platform overlooking a very busy—and very noisy—bus station. Directly in front of us was a rocky cliff with a Moslem cemetery on the top. According to our guide, these graves guarantee that the place will never be violated. The face of the cliff gave the impression of having two eyes, a nose, and a mouth. It looked eerily like a skull. We were told that hill could possibly be "Golgotha," the hill outside the old city walls (which we could see a short distance away) where Jesus was crucified. Attached to the platform was a sign reading in English, Greek and Hebrew the words:

> Then delivered he him therefore unto them to be crucified and they took Jesus and led him away. And he bearing his cross went forth into a place called Golgotha where they

crucified him, and two other with him, on either side one and Jesus in the midst.

As we stood at this holy spot, we spontaneously began singing the words of Isaac Watts' great hymn, "At the Cross."

> Alas and did my Savior bleed
> And did my Sovereign die,
> Would he devote that sacred head
> For such a one as I?
>
> At the cross, at the cross
> Where I first saw the light,
> And the burden of my heart rolled away,
> It was there by faith I received my sight and
> Now I am happy all the day.

The Meaning of Jesus' Death

This hymn of testimony expresses the sense of gratitude felt by billions of people who have found forgiveness of sins through faith in Jesus. However, many if not most have never really thought deeply about how the death of Jesus brings about the possibility of their salvation. And Christian thinkers who have thought deeply about this event throughout the centuries have not arrived at a consensus on the meaning of "the Atonement." Perhaps one reason for this lack of conformity is that the New Testament uses several metaphors, with no one metaphor fully capturing its meaning. A useful analogy for the work of Christ might be a patchwork quilt that has been stitched together from the story of Israel and its traditions with Jesus' career to form one whole. The result is that these two stories, Israel's and Jesus', become mutually interpreting.

Most of the attempts to explain the Atonement turn to the Apostle Paul. When Paul wrote to the Corinthians, he set the cross of Christ in contrast to the wisdom of "this age" and declared his intention to know nothing among them "except Jesus Christ, and him crucified." Evidently, for Paul, the cross stands at the very heart of the Christian faith. Even though it was a "stumbling block to the Jews and foolishness to Gentiles," he declared it to be the power of God and the wisdom of God (1 Cor. 1-2). This scandal means that the message of the cross stood in vivid contrast to the prevailing worldviews of Paul's day—as it does in our day. The significance of this fact may be clearly seen in the Gospels.

The Gospels and the Cross

Historically, the use of the four Gospels for atonement theology has largely been limited to a few isolated texts such as Mark 10:45—"For the Son of Man came not to be served but to serve, and to give his life a ransom for many." The implication may be that Matthew, Mark, Luke and John have little to contribute to understanding the significance of Jesus' death. Even the Apostles' Creed apparently contributes to this implication since the entire life and ministry of Jesus is absent from its affirmations. It moves from "conceived by the Holy Spirit, born of the Virgin Mary," to "suffered under Pontius Pilate, was crucified dead and buried."

Does this mean that the Gospel writers' record of Jesus' life was largely irrelevant to the real salvation meaning of the cross? Martin Kähler famously described Mark's Gospel as a "passion narrative with an extended introduction" (*The So-called Historical Jesus and the Historic, Biblical Christ*, 80 n. 11). While it is true that the bulk of the gospel narratives refer to the final days of Jesus' life, the remainder surely has a significant role to play in explaining the meaning of those last days. Because the circumstances and understanding of Jesus' death can never be torn from the fabric of the circumstances of his life, we should locate the cross within the larger context of Jesus' entire ministry. *The entire story of Jesus is crucial to an adequate understanding of his accomplishment on behalf of our salvation.*

Conflict between Love and Power

One of the most obvious characteristics of Jesus ministry was "conflict." Even before he began his public ministry, when he was an infant, conflict arose from the claims that one had been born king of the Jews. It was a claim that triggered the political jealousy of Herod that in turn resulted in tragedy for many. During the three years of his public ministry, what Jesus offered in his teaching and practice was an alternate worldview and a way of life that differed sharply from both the Roman and Jewish cultures, thus challenging both. When one confronts the prevailing culture—political or religious—in the way Jesus did, the inevitable result is conflict.

Clearly, Jesus' message crossed the grain of the Roman political order. In a similar fashion, Jesus came into conflict with the worldview of the religious elite among the Jews. The Temple was the center of an economic system of exploitation legitimated in the name of God. This system was sustained by an ideology of holiness/purity that Jesus symbolically attacked by his cleansing of the Temple and also by his repeated violation of prevailing purity concepts.

The Jewish purity system centered on "table fellowship," so purity was maintained by eating with the right people and refusing to have table fellowship with the wrong people. In a sense, what was involved was a status issue. Those with whom one ate should have the same status as oneself and therefore the same level of purity. This principle was the basis of the Pharisees' criticism of Jesus' eating with "publicans and sinners." He was acknowledging, on the basis of their own system, that the wrong people were now the right people and were being included in the kingdom he came to establish. (Luke recorded in Acts how this issue continued as a point of controversy in the early Christian communities.)

Thus, Jesus came into deadly disfavor with the prevailing worldview of Judaism. This resulted in the Jewish leaders seeking to put him to death. As in his conflict with the Romans, while he did more than offer an alternate cultural worldview, he did not do less. The implication of this alternate worldview is that those who have identified themselves by faith with the crucified Messiah are called to a life marked by *cruciformity*.

On the surface these conflicts appeared to result in the failure and defeat of Jesus' vocation; however, the truth is that his death made him the conqueror. Furthermore, his defeat of evil gave us a new concept of power. Jesus, by his death and resurrection, demonstrated that love is mightier than all other forms of power.

This conclusion leads us to the observation that, from the biblical perspective, there is a "spiritual" dimension of reality lying behind the systems that dominate and exclude the weak, the dispossessed, and the marginalized. The New Testament refers to this dimension as the "principalities and powers." (See Ephesians 3:10; 6:12; Colossians 1:13, 16)

The numerous references in the New Testament to these dark realties are complex. Every institution, culture, organization, and nation has an outward, physical manifestation and an inward, "spiritual" dimension. The earlier description of these oppressive cultural manifestations in Roman and Jewish societies at the time of Jesus serves as pertinent examples. The Temple authorities, for instance, were outward manifestations of a "power" that was their "spiritual" dimension. Since Jesus was a threat to these forces, he had to be removed. And remove him they did!

Even so, as Paul points out in 1 Corinthians, the rulers of "this age" did not understand the implications of what they were doing. If they had they would not have crucified the Lord of glory (2:8). Because of their ignorance about God's plan of salvation, they did not know that in putting Jesus to death they were actually facilitating God's plan. In his submission to their "power," marked by hate and force, he defeated them by his power of unconditional love. Paul announces that triumphant word in Colossians 3:15 in his report of the result of the cross: "He disarmed the rulers and authorities and made a public example of them, triumphing over them in it [the cross]."

The often-repeated dying words of the Roman emperor Julian the Apostate capture the significance of this "victory." After having failed to reverse the official endorsement of Christianity by the Roman Empire, he is supposed to have lamented "Thou has conquered, O pale Galilean; the world has grown grey from thy breath." The truth is however, that the "Constantinian" establishment of Christianity as the official religion of the Roman Empire actually resulted in the church surrendering the victory it had earlier gained over the "powers of this age," ultimately becoming subservient to the "spirit of the age." John Wesley emphasized this same point.

This result is why perceptive Christian theologians in recent years have expressed gratitude over the developments that have basically put an end to the endorsement of the Christian gospel by the prevailing culture. This opens the door, they argue, for the church to become once again the church and in the power of love as manifested in the cross, to challenge the "principalities and powers" that manifest themselves in the injustices and atrocities regularly demonstrated by institutions and nations.

The Significance of the Cross

Seeking to understand the significance of the cross involves confronting a variety of images in Scripture as well as the history of Christian ideas about the Atonement. The church at large has never formulated a "standard" or official explanation as it has done with the doctrines of the Trinity and the nature of Christ. People's experience of salvation reflects a wide diversity, and in the New Testament there are multiple ways of legitimately interpreting the cross that intersects with this diversity.

When it comes to "theories" of the Atonement, several shed valuable light on what God has done in Jesus Christ, but no theory is adequate in itself. This diversity is not to say that the cross can mean anything anyone wants it to mean. Obviously, some proposals fail to capture any central teaching of Scripture, and some have implications contrary to Scripture.

One touchstone of validity for any understanding of the Atonement is the nature of God. The Western church has had two views of God's essential nature: justice or love. When justice is primary, the Atonement is interpreted as a way to influence God to be willing or even able to accept the sinner. The focus is directly and even exclusively on the forgiveness of sins. When love is definitive, the Atonement is viewed as God seeking a restored relationship and initiating the restoration. John Wesley emphasized that the scripture does not say that God is justice, but it does say that God is love. This implies that a consistent Wesleyan interpretation of the Atonement would avoid an understanding that makes Jesus' death a means of satisfying God's justice. Furthermore, when the emphasis of the Eastern Church on the transforming implication of the Incarnation is factored in, as John Wesley did, the result is a full-orbed understanding of the Atonement. This two-fold emphasis addresses the full problem of sin, providing for both forgiveness and sanctification.

It is this bountiful provision about which Horatio G. Spafford wrote in his hymn, "It is Well with my Soul":

> My sin—oh, the bliss of this glorious tho't!
> My sin—not in part but the whole
> Is nailed to His cross and I bear it no more
> Praise the Lord, praise the Lord, O my soul!

This Wesleyan emphasis is consistent with the biblical witness. From the Lord God's return to Eden following Adam's disobedience to the dramatic picture of God's redeeming love in the experience of Hosea, the Old Testament always depicts the divine relation to humanity in terms of compassionate love. One by one, the stories of human rebellion in Genesis 3—11 indicate that the human tendency toward sin is not matched by God's withdrawal. In fact, the Scriptures as a whole provide no ground for a portrait of an angry God needing to be appeased in atoning sacrifice. This fact is not to deny the recurring element of judgment, but it is fair to say that it is redemptive rather than retributive. The book of Hosea makes this point explicitly. The Lord indicates his intention to take away the fertility of the land that Israel had come to attribute to Baal. Why? It was for the purpose of bringing his people to their senses so that they would return to him as the true source of their well being (see Hosea 2:5-20).

Everything in the four Gospels shouts that God's love reaches out for the lost, the last, and the least. Paul puts the matter beyond dispute in Romans 5: "For while we were still weak, at the right time Christ died for the ungodly.... But God proves his love for us in that while we still were sinners Christ died for us.... For while we were enemies, we were reconciled to God through the death of his Son" (vv. 6, 8, 10). No other conclusion can be drawn in the light of the biblical text most familiar to the average Christian, John 3:16.

REFLECTIONS

If the definitive motive of the atoning work of God in Christ is love, the question is this: how does love bring about reconciliation? Among the various metaphors in the New Testament, one stands out, the one that emerged in the earthly ministry of Jesus: the metaphor of conflict and conquest. Among the metaphors from the Old Testament used to explain the work of Christ, the Exodus takes a prominent place. Throughout the Old Testament the Israelites repeatedly expressed hope for a new exodus that would bring about the same result as the original event—deliverance of God's people from bondage both externally and internally.

An essential aspect of the Exodus was breaking the will of Pharaoh by demonstrating the power of Yahweh over the "power" of the gods of Egypt. The ten plagues accomplished this objective. This same approach was implied by Jesus in his response to those who accused him of casting out demons by the power of Beelzebub, the ruler of demons: "If it is by the finger of God that I cast out the demons, then the kingdom of God has come to you" (Lk. 11:20). Matthew reports Jesus' reference as being to the "Spirit of God" (Matt. 12:28). Scholars have reasoned that Luke's report was probably the actual words of Jesus while Matthew's was an interpretation. Where did the reference to the "finger of God" come from? When the Egyptian sorcerers were unable to duplicate the fourth plague, they confessed to Pharaoh, "[I]t is the finger of God." Jesus' healings, especially the exorcisms, were evidences that a divine power like that at the Exodus was breaking into history, the power of love that would set prisoners free.

The heart of the Christian gospel is news about God and about Jesus; news that this Jesus had become the spearhead of God's "age to come"; news that, within this new age, the principalities and powers, including earthly rulers, the powers of darkness, and sin and death themselves had been defeated and were now summoned to allegiance. Charles Wesley loved to celebrate this salvation truth and repeated it in more than one of his hymns:

> Long my imprison'd spirit lay,
> Fast bound in sin and nature's night.
> Thine eye diffused a quickening ray,
> The dungeon flamed with light.
> My chains fell off, my heart was free
> I rose went forth and followed Thee.[43]

Stand with me again before the place of the Skull and know that the love of God has reached out in redeeming and rescuing love—even to you and me! Isaac Watt's hymn provides a most appropriate response to the cross:

> When I survey the wondrous cross
> On which the Prince of Glory died,
> My richest gain I count but loss,
>   and pour contempt on all my pride.
>
> Were the whole realm of nature mine,
>   That were a present far too small.
> Love so amazing, so divine,
> Demands my soul, my life, my all!

---

[43]"And Can it Be?"

Questions to Think About

1. What is the problem with saying that Jesus' death on the cross appeased the wrath of God?
2. How should the cross influence our discipleship?
3. How does the message of the cross address the needs of people who are enslaved by an addiction?
4. How does this interpretation of the death of Jesus influence your participation in the Lord's Supper?

Chapter Thirteen

MOUNT OF ASCENSION

Revelation of the Current Rule of Christ

When he had said this, as they were watching, he was lifted up, and a cloud took him out of their sight. When he was going and they were gazing up toward heaven, suddenly two men in white robes stood by them. They said, "Men of Galilee, why do you stand looking up toward heaven? This Jesus who has been taken up from you into heaven will come in the same way as you saw him go into heaven" (Acts 1:9-11).

Mount of Olives

The most universally accepted Christian creed, The Apostles' Creed, affirms the belief that Jesus Christ "ascended into heaven where he sits at the right hand of God, the Father Almighty." Unlike some of the other affirmations of the Creed, this belief is explicitly taught in only two statements of Scripture, both from the work of Luke. One is in his Gospel (24:50-53) and the other in the Book of Acts, quoted above. A third reference is found in Mark 16:19, but since it is not found in the oldest and best manuscripts there is consensus that this reference is a later addition without canonical authority. However, other New Testament passages seem to imply it (Jn. 3:13; 6:62; 20:17; Rom. 10:6-7; Eph.1:20; 4:8-10; Heb. 4:14; 9:24; 1 Peter 3:22). The scripture record does not identify the place where the ascension occurred but early church tradition placed it on the Mount of Olives.

The ascension has significant theological implications when interpreted in the context of the total Christ event, Even so, in recent centuries it has been common for this event to be given relatively little attention in comparison with the cross and resurrection. Furthermore, it is generally given short shrift in most works of systematic theology.

Cosmology and the Ascension

Prior to the emergence of the modern scientific knowledge of cosmology, the early theologians of the church, from both east and west, preached at great length on the subject. While the sixteenth century Protestant Reformers often did so in very sensitive and lively fashion, one does not often hear a sermon on the ascension today. One reason for this post-Enlightenment neglect of the ascension is that the special imagery of the story—its assumption of a three-story universe—seems at complete odds with our modern knowledge.

It is true that to the literal-minded person, reading the account in Acts raises some interesting cosmological questions. Somewhat crudely put, one might ask, "did Jesus become the first space traveler?" This question only arises, however, if one assumes that heaven is a place within our space-time universe. This view was apparently the assumption of Uri Gagarin, the Russian cosmonaut who returned from his visit in space and declared that he did not see God up there, so God must not exist. Of course, one could argue like a deeply devout lady of my acquaintance—"he didn't go out far enough!" If her argument were valid, Jesus is located so distant from our world that he has no immediate relation to us. It also calls into question the "omnipresence" of God.

Neither of these are satisfactory conclusions. However, influential theologians from the past did not fall into this crass literalism. In commenting on Ephesians 4:10, John Calvin said, "When Christ is said to be in heaven we must not view him as dwelling among the spheres and numbering the stars.... Not that it is literally a place beyond the world, but we cannot speak of the kingdom of God without using our ordinary language." We think and speak only in terms of what we know or can conceive based on the structure of our minds. Actually, we cannot speak literally at all of God as if he were an object that is subject to space and time categories except by analogy.

It is our natural tendency to think about both God and heaven in terms of "up." But "up" is relative to the position of the earth as it rotates. What is "up" to some is "down" to others. Our present knowledge of space makes such concepts unintelligible. This phenomenon is why William Barclay could say that the "Ascension" is the most difficult incident in the life of Jesus either to visualize or to understand. Graphic attempts to portray it in films or paintings only result in making it appear absurd. What then shall we say?

Other than the unacceptable option of declaring it a myth with no historical reality, perhaps the answer is to be found in a more adequate concept of "heaven." Although not new with him, N. T. Wright has popularized an explanation that avoids the cosmological problem of speaking about heaven in space-time categories and appears to be consistent with both Scripture and our modern cosmological knowledge. He proposes that we think of heaven as "God's space" or "realm." It is not a "place" in our space/time continuum like Nashville or Philadelphia, even though the symbolic language (like "streets of gold") that is sometimes applied to it sounds quite solid.

God's realm is a dimension of reality that is, in a sense, all around us. We are separated from God's space, not by miles of physical space, but by what may be described figuratively as a "veil," which can sometimes become so thin that it seems heaven and earth intersect and interlock. Hugh Stowell expresses the possibility and reality of this truth in his hymn about "the mercy seat."

> There, there, on eagles' wings we soar,
> And time and sense seem all no more;
> And heaven comes down, our souls to greet,
> And glory crowns the mercy seat.

In support of conceiving heaven this way, Wright calls attention to the language often used in Scripture about the second advent: "when he shall *appear*" (1 Jn. 3:2, KJV). This expression does not suggest that Jesus comes from some physical distance far away. Rather, when the veil of our human blindness is drawn back, he simply appears and it looks as if he has come from somewhere else. It is much like the experience of Elisha's servant reported in 2 Kings 6:17—"Then Elisha prayed: 'O Lord, please open his eyes that he may see. So the Lord opened the eyes of the servant, and he saw; the mountain was full of horses and chariots of fire all around Elisha." This way of conceptualizing heaven is a very comforting thought and many Christians have found it inspiring. I shared it with a group of senior citizens in a retirement center and they responded positively. I very tentatively suggest that this view may be a reasonable explanation for the occasional reports of "near death" experiences. For a moment the "veil" was drawn back and there was a glimpse of the beyond.

Important Theological Meanings

One of the central questions regarding the ascension of Jesus concerns its relation to his resurrection. There certainly is a clear distinction between them in theological meaning as well as in historical fact. It is one thing to assert that Jesus had been raised from death: it is another thing (however closely connected) to assert that he now shares in the sovereignty of God over heaven and earth.

In light of the general New Testament emphasis on the resurrection of Jesus as his exaltation (Lk. 9:51; Acts 1:2, 22; Rom. 1:2; Phil. 2:9-11), we agree with John Maile that the ascension narratives "can and should be seen as conforming to the resurrection/exaltation pattern of the rest of the New Testament in describing the final departure of the *already exalted* Lord."[44] The question then becomes, what is the significance of this departure?

It is important in answering this question to be certain that we understand the real nature of the resurrection of Jesus. Popular religion tends to individualize its meaning in terms of one's personal existence: Jesus was raised from the dead so I too have hope of being raised from the dead. This implication is gloriously true, but the resurrection has a far deeper meaning. We must recall that Jesus began his ministry, as did John the Baptist, with the announcement that the kingdom of God was "at hand." Throughout the ministry of Jesus, including in his parables and deeds and particularly his healings, there were indicators that the kingdom had invaded history in his person and work.

Note the significance of the response of Jesus to accusations made against him: "If it is by the finger of God that I cast out the demons, then the kingdom of God has come to you" (Lk. 11:20). Throughout his entire ministry, those he had chosen to "be with him" stubbornly failed to recognize the direction his ministry was taking. As a result, when he

---

[44]John F. Maile, "The Ascension in Luke-Acts," *Tyndale Bulletin* 37 (1986):48. Emphasis added.

was arrested and put to death their expectations were crushed. Recall the disconsolate pair on the road to Emmaus! The answer to their disillusionment offered by the unrecognized Jesus puts the entire matter into perspective. "Was it not necessary that the Messiah would suffer these things and then enter into his glory?" (Lk. 24: 26).

The resurrection of Jesus was the validation that God's history-long plan to redeem the world through Israel, now embodied in "one faithful Israelite," had reached its climax. The kingdom of God had now invaded history with Jesus as the exalted King. The new creation had begun, the "age to come" had dawned, the exile had ended, and God had fulfilled his promises to Abraham. This truth united early Christianity beyond their diversity. They told, and lived, a form of Israel's story that reached its climax in Jesus and which then issued in their Spirit-empowered new life and task. Or put another way, first century Jews looked forward to a public event in and through which their God would reveal to the entire world that he was not just a local tribal deity, but the creator and sovereign of all. The early Christians looked back to an event in and through which, they claimed Israel's God had done exactly that. *The ascension of Jesus, then, was the enthronement of the King following his conquest of evil and the establishment of his kingdom.*

Another important aspect of the resurrection for understanding the meaning of the ascension is the fact that it was a "bodily" resurrection. It is easy to fall into thinking about a spiritual resurrection in which Jesus' "soul" survives or revived after apparent death, but this way of thinking is totally contrary to the biblical hope of immortality, which is always an embodied immortality. Jesus had not been resuscitated as had Lazarus or the son of the widow of Nain or Jairus' daughter.

His Resurrection was not a return to the former bodily existence that was mortal and would face death again. Jesus had passed through death and out the other side into *a new order of being*. Paul struggles to explain this phenomenon in 1 Corinthians 15 by describing it as a "spiritual body." What Paul means is not a body made out of non-physical spirit, but a physical body animated by the Spirit, a Spirit-*driven* body.

This interpretation means that Jesus' ascension was the entrance of his glorified body into heaven. Jesus departed in order to be present with his followers everywhere. A physical body would be localized in one place. But his departure as a resurrected, glorified "spiritual body" is the possibility that "his spirit" would now be available in an omnipresent fashion. Furthermore, the significance of this aspect of the ascension points to the reality of the final resurrection of the saints as a bodily resurrection. The Apostles' Creed recognizes the distinctive feature of the biblical hope for the future in the words "the resurrection of the body." A disembodied immortality is not biblical.

Aside from the simple fact that the ascension was Jesus' final departure from being physically present to his followers, we need to say a word about the significance of the forty days between the resurrection and the ascension. Since his disciples had never recognized the radical worldview transformation that was occurring in Jesus' ministry and death prior to the resurrection, there was need to convince them of the reality of the resurrection and teach them about the kingdom of God as it must now be understood. They could no longer think of it in ethnic terms or as a political entity composed only of Abraham's descendents according to the flesh. These implications had to be nailed down in that interim period.

Jesus' Inaugurated Kingship

What then is the theological significance of the ascension? Since John Calvin and his *Institutes* Protestant theology has widely used the offices of Prophet, Priest and King as the standard template for understanding the ministry of Christ, including his post-resurrection work. Jesus was Prophet (his public ministry), Priest (his suffering and death), and King (confirmed by his resurrection and ascension). While the ascension is the confirmation of the exaltation of Christ and his present lordship, it is also the inauguration of his continuing kingship. Anyone living in the Roman world of the first century would recognize this meaning of ascension.

The early church fathers recognized the importance of this truth. Cyril of Jerusalem highlighted it in his summary of the entire scheme of redemption: "In Bethlehem He descended from heaven; from the Mount of Olives He ascended into heaven. In Bethlehem He came to men to begin the work of Redemption; from the Mount of Olives He ascended to receive the crown for the work of Redemption." These two movements are intimately related. Joseph Haroutunian points out the implication of this interconnectedness: "no one aspect of the mission of Christ can be stated properly without reference to the others. If Christ died, but did not rise again, our faith is vain. If he rose but did not ascend, he is not gone to God the Father Almighty, he is somewhere in our world; he must be truly a 'wandering Jew.' If he is not on the right hand of God the Father, he does not reign, and we have no King."

A simple parable may be helpful. Imagine a country in which the population is under the dominion of a small but powerful group who holds them in virtual slavery. They have neither the resources nor ability to throw off the yoke that keeps them in submission. Then there comes to that country a stranger with a few friends who take pity on their plight. They have both the resources and ability to break the stranglehold the ruling powers have on the population. Now, for the first time in memory, they are free! Suppose the liberator then moves elsewhere, leaving the people to maintain their liberated situation. But the previous ruling group reasserts itself and regains the power they had lost. What had been accomplished would have been in vain.

But suppose instead that the liberator accepts the role of ruler and remains in the country, thus maintaining long-term the new situation that his action had brought about. This scenario seems to be the significance of the ascension of Jesus. He "went away" bodily so that he could be universally present in the Spirit. The liberator is now seated at the right hand of God and continues to rule in the new creation that his death and resurrection has brought into reality. Herein lays the importance of the ongoing kingship of Jesus, the ascended Messiah. In a word, the ascension of Jesus is the historical attestation of the reality of Christ's ongoing lordship.

Ongoing Intercession

The function of Jesus at the "right hand" of the Father is identified by the author of Hebrews as "intercession." (Heb. 7:25). What is the meaning of this "intercession?" The idea of intercession could imply the incompleteness of the atonement of Christ, that something more is needed in order to make acceptance available to humanity. At least no Protestant would believe this, nor would the New Testament. God does not have to be persuaded to love us by Christ dying for us *and* praying for us. It was because God loved the world so much that he sent his Son in the first place. Similarly, when Christ prays for us he is not trying to persuade an unwilling and unloving God to take pity on us. We must not imagine that, because Christ continues to intercede for us, somehow the atonement was incomplete.

Hebrews 4:14 links Jesus' priesthood to his ascension: "Since, then, we have a great high priest who has passed through the heavens, Jesus, the Son of God; let us hold fast to our confession." A proper understanding of the Book of Hebrews will shed considerable light on the significance of Christ's intercession in heaven. First, and of supreme importance, we must recognize the purpose of the letter. Its intention is to shore up the faith of Jewish converts to the Christian faith who are being sorely tested and thus tempted to return to a Jewish faith lacking Jesus as the fulfilling Messiah. The writer is seeking to show the superiority of the Christian way by emphasizing its better priesthood and sacrifice. In doing so he is appropriating the sacrificial theology of the Old Testament, particularly as described in Leviticus, emphasizing its fulfillment in Christ.

It is essential to recognize that the Levitical sacrifices functioned within the covenant relation. That is why, despite its many complexities, the work of atonement [in Hebrews] had a distinctly pastoral function. They do not serve to establish one's relation to God, a relation established solely on the basis of God's grace. This truth is clearly exemplified in the covenant Yahweh made with Abraham (Gen. 15). The proper function of sacrifice is implied by the Hebrews' writer in his recognition that there is no sacrifice for "willful or high-handed sin" (Heb. 10:26), which may be forgiven upon repentance. Rather the sacrifices in Leviticus and the sacrificial aspect of Christ's atonement being emphasized in Hebrews are for "unintentional or unwitting sin," any deviation from the perfect law.

This purpose is how the sacrifices offered in the tabernacle (or Temple) functioned. They had to be offered regularly. They were incomplete and needed to be repeated. This need for repetition is why the Hebrews writer makes the point that the priest offered them while "standing" (Heb. 10:11). By contrast, when Jesus offered himself as a sacrifice (not for willful sin but for those ongoing, inevitable imperfections in finite, fallen life), "he sat down" (10:12). This description makes perfect sense in light of the writer's purpose. How much "better" the sacrifice of Christ!

Theologically, we can conclude from this analysis that the intercession of Christ in heaven is a symbol for the ongoing provision for the "cleansing from (unwitting) sin" celebrated in 1 John 1:9. We do not need to offer another sacrifice, and neither does the Son need to persuade the Father to accept us in our shortcomings. As we walk in the light with faith and integrity, "the blood cleanses [present tense] from all sin."

Ascension and the Church

The ascension of Jesus is the essential link between the life of Jesus and the life of the church. This relation involves two movements, both of which Luke emphasizes in Acts. First--and prior to his leaving them--Jesus gave to his followers a commission to carry out the mission of extending the kingdom by implementing the work that he had done. They were not to do again what he had done, indeed they could not. They were to build on the foundation he had laid in his victory over evil. Second, Jesus promised them the power and authority to carry out this mission by the gift of the Holy Spirit, which they received on the Day of Pentecost. And so it happened! As the epigrammatic way of putting it says:

> Jesus went up!
> The Holy Spirit came down!
> And the church went out!

The ascension is the event by which Jesus decisively ended his time on earth in terms of his physical presence by returning to the place from which he had come. This departure doubtless occurred in climactic fashion so that the disciples might know that it was the end of one chapter in their relation to the risen Jesus and the beginning of another. There would have been something indecisive about the resurrection appearances had they just slowly faded out.

The departure carried Jesus out of the disciples' sight by a "cloud." The "cloud" was obviously not some sort of supernatural spaceship but the traditional symbol of the presence of God into which Jesus was entering. This symbolism was used throughout the Old Testament from Israel's experience in the wilderness to the inauguration of Solomon's Temple. But it is also a symbol of the hiddenness of Christ subsequent to his earthly life. John Calvin pointed out that the cloud was a needed bridle to our curiosity—a reminder of the distance between God and humans, a reminder that we only see in part and only know in part.

Nevertheless, we are not thereby left with total mystery. We have signposts pointing into the cloud, signposts that have been planted solidly in our space-time world by the Incarnation. This function means that the life and ministry of Jesus "at the right hand of God" is fully informed by his life "among us." The Incarnation was not a temporary visitation of God into human existence prior to withdrawing again into remoteness. God is forever the God of the Incarnation. The Jesus who was here is the same Jesus who now is there.

Although not specifically mentioning the ascension, several New Testament passages that speak of his lordship imply it. For instance: 1 Corinthians 15:25, "For he must reign until he has put all his enemies under his feet;" Philippians 2:9, "Therefore God has highly exalted him and bestowed on him the name which is above every name, that at the name of Jesus every knee should bow. . . and every tongue confess that Jesus Christ is Lord;" Ephesians 1:20, ". . . which he accomplished in Christ when he raised him from the dead and seated him at his right hand in the heavenly places."

The affirmation of Jesus' lordship poses a difficulty faced by the original disciples and now confronts us. It involves how we understand the significance of that lordship now being exercised from heaven in the light of the continuing reality of evil in this world. Can we imagine what a shock his departure must have been for those early disciples? They had expected him to establish his kingdom on earth immediately—and instead he went away! Note this analysis of the problem:

> This is something that we can surely understand, because it is true for us, too, that Christ is no longer on this earth. The shock the disciples felt we can still feel today. Has not our faith been jolted time and again by the realization that there is so little evidence of the power of this Christ in our world? The same question arises to plague the believer today, and the unbeliever triumphantly throws it into his face: *"Where now is your God?"* This is what prevents so many, many people from believing—that there is no evidence of God's power to say nothing of his love, upon the earth.[45]

Is this pessimism justified? It certainly is very common.

A more positive response calls attention to signs of new creation that have appeared throughout Christian history. It is true that evil is still rampant in our world. Rather than being gloomy because of this continuance, however, the disciples departed from the "launch point" (Jesus' ascension) with the intention of becoming prepared to carry out the implications of Jesus' lordship in their world. They and we are now

---

[45]H.W. Bartsch, "The Meaning of the Ascension," *The Lutheran Quarterly*, February 1954, 45.

living in the time between the "no longer" (the old order has been superseded) and the "not yet" (the full consummation of the new order).

As Karl Barth once said, as the empty grave makes us look down to see the end of one age, so the ascension makes us look up to see what is to come. John Wesley emphasizes the optimism of the grace that comes to us from the power of the risen and exalted Christ. He describes as follows the results of his own ministry:

> What have been the consequences . . . of the doctrines I have preached for nine years last past? By the fruits shall ye know those of whom I speak; even the cloud of witnesses, who at this hour experience the gospel which I preach to be the power of God unto salvation. The habitual drunkard that was, is now temperate in all things; the whoremonger now flees fornication; he that stole, steals no more, but works with his hands; he that cursed or swore perhaps at every sentence, has now learned to serve the Lord with fear, and rejoice unto him with reverence, these formerly enslaved to various habits of sin are now brought to uniform habits of holiness.[46]

The Ascension and Worship

There are further implications of the ascension for the life of the church. The Eastern Orthodox tradition has strongly emphasized the relation between the ascension and worship. It stresses that in the liturgy of the church the presence of Christ is known. Although normally not relying as heavily on liturgy, evangelical congregations likewise experience the presence of the risen Christ since Jesus said that where his people are gathered in his name, he would be there.

Historically there has been much theological discussion about the presence of Christ in the Lord's Supper (Eucharist). During the Reformation period debate raged around the issue of the "bodily presence of Christ." Luther attempted to take literally the words of Jesus in instituting the Supper, "this is my body." He rejected the idea of an

---

[46]*Works*, 8:494-5. The church I attend experiences a regular flow of folk being baptized who have been delivered from various forms of addiction by the grace and transforming power of Jesus. Perhaps this is what Daniel Steele meant when he suggested that the "greater works" of the disciples was "miracles of the Holy Ghost." *The Gospel of the Comforter*.

actual transformation of the bread into the body of Christ (the Catholic view), but held that the Christ is really, bodily present as the sacramental elements are received in faith.

By some contrast, John Calvin opted for a spiritual presence. John Wesley's view is similar, rejecting any bodily presence, but insisting on a *spiritual presence.* Our emphasis should be on a *real* presence as opposed to a mere memorial—a symbolic meal together as believers that only reverently remembers Jesus. The ascended Christ really does remain among his children. The focus of the ascension should be on the *presence* and not the absence of Jesus! He went—and came in the continuing presence of the Spirit—in order that disciples of all time could be empowered to carry on his mission in this world.

The ascension emphasizes the importance of and the empowerment of the church for mission. The angel asks the wondering disciples, "Why are you standing there looking into the sky?" What were they looking for? One might speculate that they might be looking for an immediate reappearing since the angel had indicated a return. If so, this point is an implicit rebuke of those who are so preoccupied with the so-called "signs of the times" and the fulfillment of prophecy in the morning headlines that they neglect the main thing.

The return of Christ is crucially important, but to become "cloud gazers" is to fail to "occupy" until he comes back. The disciples did the appropriate thing. They returned to Jerusalem with joy, worshipping Christ and spreading the gospel with one eye on the mission and one on the sky. The upward look empowered them for the outward mission.

REFLECTIONS

Those of us who live in the western world and have been influenced by the 18th century Enlightenment will have difficulty recognizing the radical implications of the Ascension for our relation to the so-called secular world. The 18th century Enlightenment proposed a split-level world that separated religion and politics and resulted, in America, in a separation of church and state. (At least in principle). However, anyone in the ancient world hearing about an "ascension" would immediately recognize that someone was being elevated to kingship and thus to absolute authority over the whole realm. I grew up hearing it said that Jesus must be Lord of all or he would not be Lord at all but did not understand that it meant the whole of life and every area of life, not just the "religious" dimensions.

This Enlightenment assumption has had two major results. Religion and faith have become privatized; religion is defined as what one does with his/her solitariness. The other related assumption is that religion has no place in the public square. But when Jesus came announcing that the Kingdom of God had drawn near everybody knew that God's kingdom didn't refer to a place, perhaps a place called heaven, where God ruled and to which God's people would be gathered, well away from the wicked world, at the end of their lives. God's kingdom was the rule of God, and Jesus said that people should pray for it to come on earth as in heaven; and here he was, on earth, making it happen before people's very eyes. When Herod heard about it, he understood its implication and was angry; he was King of the Jews, and rival claimants tended not to live long. When the chief priests heard, they knew that it meant a challenge to their power base, the Temple. If Caesar had heard, he would have reacted similarly.

When Paul wrote his letter to the Romans, he introduced his message by using the key terms of the Caesar-cult, which was the fastest growing religion of the Empire. The accession of the emperor, and also his birthday, was hailed as *euaggelion*, good news or gospel. The emperor was the *kyrios*, the lord of the world, the one who claimed the allegiance and loyalty of subjects throughout his wide empire. When he came in person to pay a state visit to a colony or province, the word for his royal presence was *Parousia*, one term used for Jesus' second coming. In declaring at the royal capital that he was not ashamed of the "gospel of Christ," Paul was deliberately affirming the lordship of Jesus over Caesar.

This, of course, was simply drawing out the implications of the Messianic hope. Isaiah had declared, "Unto us a child is born, unto us a son is given and the government shall be upon his shoulders." (Isa. 9:6) We elect new leaders with great optimism and place upon their shoulders burdens that they are unable to bear. The only one who is capable of bringing justice to the world is the crucified and risen Jesus of Nazareth, God's Messiah, Lord of the world; he is already reigning at God's right hand; he will reappear to complete this rule by abolishing all enemies, including sin and death themselves. The classic statement of this "good news" is Paul's word in 1 Corinthians 15 that "he must reign until he has put all his enemies under his feet. The last enemy to be destroyed is death. For God has put all things in subjection under his feet."

Questions to Think About

1. What is the danger of too narrow a focus on the second coming of Christ?
2. What is the relation between the heavenly ministry of Christ and the work of the Holy Spirit?
3. How can the book of Hebrews' emphasis on Jesus as high priest help us understand how the ascended Christ can be "touched with the feeling our infirmities?"
4. How does the interpretation of the meaning of heaven as presented in this chapter make God's presence more real?

Chapter Fourteen

MOUNT OF FINAL VISION

Revelation of the New Creation

> Then I saw a new heaven and a new earth; for the first heaven and the first earth had passed away, and the sea was no more. And I saw the holy city, the New Jerusalem, coming down out of heaven from God prepared as a bride adorned for her husband.... Then one of the seven angels who had the seven bowls full of the seven last plagues came and said to me, "Come, I will show you the bride, the wife of the Lamb." And in the spirit he carried me away to **a great, high mountain** and showed me the holy city Jerusalem coming down out of heaven from God (Rev. 21:1-3; 9-10).

Over the years, I have occasionally heard it said that the Book of Revelation was not intended to be understood. While parts of it are particularly difficult to interpret because of its extensive symbolism, it does declare itself to be a "revelation," a disclosure (Rev. 1:1). The writer intended to communicate an intelligible, meaningful message to a specific historic situation. Rather than being of merely historic interest however, it continues to be a disclosure and indeed is intended to be understood.

Both Then and Now

Few have questioned that the message of Revelation was directed to a situation of either persecution or impending persecution that was threatening the Christian church over the issue of emperor worship. Nonetheless, the historical setting and the message of the ultimate end of the age are mingled. The climactic events of human history are seen in and through the immediate historical situation of the first century. If the initial application of the book to the problem of emperor worship in the first century exhausted the meaning of this revelation, it would have only an antiquarian interest for us. However, its application is not limited to that—it continues to have revelatory significance for us. How can both of these claims be justified?

The fact that the dynamics of one historical event foreshadows the final struggle becomes the basis for the possibility of a fresh understanding in every age. John's prophecy can repeatedly relate to situations in subsequent times that are illuminated by his descriptions and vision rooted in the past. Nevertheless, this relation does not allow us to make a one-to-one correlation between the prophecy and any historical crisis subsequent to the original one. Any contemporary application must always be grounded in the past, which then sheds light on the present.

In the climactic vision of the book upon which this chapter focuses, the prayer Jesus taught his disciples to pray--and that many of us pray every Lord's Day in worship--has reached its fulfillment: "Thy will be done on earth as it is in heaven." John's vision of the "New Jerusalem" coming to earth was the means of expressing, in symbolic theological terms, the meaning of his revelation of the nature of God's goal for this world, the coming to earth of the kingdom of God. Everything that God had intended in his original creation of the "heavens and the earth," including his creation of humanity in the image of God, has been finally actualized.

Three Endings, One Beginning

John's vision from the "high mountain" involves the consummation of all history and then a new beginning. Because of this, we should not really speak of it as "final." The consummation has at least four aspects.

1. The End of Evil. From the beginning of the creation, God's purposes had been threatened by an opposing force. It was provisionally overcome through the ordering word of the Creator: "In the beginning when God created the heavens and the earth, the earth was a formless void and darkness covered the face of the deep, while a wind from God swept over the face of the waters. Then God said. . ." (Gen. 1:1-3a). For the Hebrew faith, this act of creation was the beginning of history. In emphasizing this originating event, the biblical tradition makes use of traditional motifs that once circulated in pagan contexts but gave them a completely different meaning. This new meaning results, in part, from the fact that ancient myths refer to recurrent events, such as the seasons of the year, whereas in the biblical understanding of history, events are one of a kind and are non-repeatable.

In one Babylonian myth, the god Marduk engaged in a battle with Tiamat, the female personification of the powers of chaos. In Genesis the Hebrew word translated as "deep" in Genesis 1:2 is the word *tehom*, which has a linguistic relation to the Babylonian *Tiamat*. Moreover, since the Genesis text begins by portraying a pre-creation condition of watery chaos, the sea and/or the sea monster (leviathan) became the symbol for evil in the Hebrew worldview. This symbolism is reinforced by the fact that the Hebrews apparently had a built-in fear of the sea, possibly because they had always been inland dwellers. When Solomon began international trade, he had to hire Phoenician sailors to operate his shipping fleet.

By the use of this symbolism throughout the Bible, creation is pictured as constantly threatened by chaos. In the great flood of Noah's time, there was a new outbreak of the waters of chaos, a cosmic catastrophe that threatened to return the earth to its pre-creation condition. The covenant established in Genesis 9:16 signified by the rainbow was God's unconditional promise, guaranteed by his word, that never again would the waters of chaos inundate human history with *total* disorder. The new beginning was essentially re-creation.

This promise informed the picture John sees after being "caught up" to heaven (Rev. 4:1-3).There he was shown "what must take place after this," namely the series of events that would bring world history to its consummation. He saw the throne, the seat of authority, surrounded by a "rainbow that looked like an emerald." This revelation implies the assurance of the faithfulness of God to his word. The events that were apparently occurring or about to occur in the Roman Empire of John's time would not totally destroy the church—despite all appearance to the contrary

The symbolism of "the sea" not only had corporate but also personal reference. In the sufferings of Job, his own personal existence and any meaning that life might have, was being threatened. His whole worldview was coming unraveled. Sometimes almost irreverently, he challenged God to explain what was happening. The Lord reminded him that oftentimes the reality of evil is beyond our finite capacity to understand, so we have to trust in the dark. God uses the symbolism of the sea and related imagery to emphasize the futility of Job's insistence on complete understanding.

God says to Job, "Can you draw out Leviathan with a fishhook, or press down its tongue with a cord? Can you put a rope in its nose, or pierce its jaw with a hook? Will it make many supplications to you? Will it speak soft words to you? Will it make a covenant with you to be taken as your servant forever? Will you play with it as with a bird, or will you put it on leash for your girls? Lay hands on it; think of the battle; you will not do it again! Any hope of capturing it will be disappointed; were not even the gods overwhelmed at the sight of it? No one is so fierce as to dare to stir it up. Who can stand before it? Who can confront it and be safe?--under the whole heaven, who?" (Job 41:1-11).

Job got the point! He recognized that if he tried to domesticate evil by fully understanding it he would have hooked a fish that he could not land. He would have launched his intellectual boat on a sea that he could not navigate. So he submitted in humble trust. If he never understood, God knew what was going on: "Then Job answered the Lord: I know that you can do all things, and that no purpose of yours can be thwarted. Who is this that hides counsel without knowledge? Therefore, I have uttered what I did not understand, things too wonderful for me, which I did not know. Hear, and I will speak; I will question you, and you declare to me. I had heard of you by the hearing of the ear, but now my eye sees you; therefore, I despise myself and repent in dust and ashes" (Job 42:1-6).

On the world scene, when it seemed that the kingdom of God was going to be swallowed up in the power games of world empires, God gave Daniel a vision of hope: "In the first year of King Belshazzar of Babylon, Daniel had a dream and visions of his head as he lay in bed. When he wrote down the dream: I, Daniel, saw in my vision by night the four winds of heaven stirring up the great sea, and four great beasts came up out of the sea, different from one another." (Dan. 7:1-3) Like his other visions, these beasts "out of the sea" were threatening the very existence of the people of God. They represented the nations that were apparently about to eclipse Israel, particularly the Seleucid nation under the kingship of Antiochus Epiphanes.

Evil often threatens, but the forces of chaos represented by the beasts out of the sea (kingdoms) were not going to accomplish their intention. Daniel saw the ultimate triumph of the kingdom of God: "I saw one like a human being coming with the clouds of heaven. And he came to the Ancient One and was presented before him. To him was given dominion and glory and kingship, that all people, nations, and languages should serve him. His dominion is an everlasting dominion that shall not pass away, and his kingship is one that shall never be destroyed" (Dan. 7:13-14). This vision sustained the Jewish people through difficult times until one named Jesus identified himself with the "Son of Man" of Daniel 7 and established the kingdom by his own death and resurrection.

It was the faith of the people of God that, even though chaos threatened, God would hold back the sea, the sea monster, the destructive forces from overwhelming his people. They had seen that faith become reality at the Red Sea when God divided the waters and enabled them to escape the army of Egypt. In their worship they celebrated both the initial and the continued victory of the Lord over the chaos-monster, the sea: "When the waters saw you, O God, when the waters saw you, they were afraid; the very deep trembled. The clouds poured out water, the skies thundered; your arrows flashed on every side. The crash of your thunder was in the whirlwind; your lightnings lit up the world; the earth trembled and shook. Your way was through the sea, your path through the mighty waters; yet your footprints were unseen. You led your people like a flock by the hand of Moses and Aaron" (Ps. 77:16-20).

Such faith sustained the individual when life came crashing in: "Save me, O God, for the waters have come up to my neck. I sink in deep mire where there is no foothold. I have come into deep waters, and the flood sweeps over me. I am weary with my crying; my throat is parched. My eyes grow dim with waiting for my God" (Psalm 69:1-3). A similar confidence is heard in the classic words of John Rippon:

> When thro' the deep waters I call thee to go,
> The rivers of sorrow shall not overflow;
> For I will be with thee thy trials to bless
> And sanctify to thee thy deepest distress.

On such an assurance the church is built—and will be sustained, no matter what. This picture is the wonderful view that one can see with John from the mount of the final revelation.

The Jewish hope also included the expectation that the time would come when the Lord would ultimately abolish the threatening chaos: "On that day the Lord with his cruel and great and strong sword will punish Leviathan the fleeing serpent, Leviathan the twisting serpent, and he will kill the dragon that is in the sea" (Isa. 27:1). The awful evil will finally experience its own death.

When we come to the New Testament, we hear the good news that God in Christ has won the decisive victory over all the powers of evil, death, and darkness. The sea is drained and Leviathan is dead! The uniqueness of John's vision is not that the ultimate victory over evil will be won at the climax or end of the historical process. It sees the victory over evil having taken place at the *mid-point* of history in the death and resurrection of Christ. In the vision given John at the threshold of the events that bring about the final consummation, the only one who is qualified to open the seals and thus bring about the outcome is the "slain Lamb." Jesus had been slaughtered. Nevertheless, he was the one who "has conquered, so that he can open the scroll and its seven seals" (Rev. 5:5-6).

While it was clear that evil had met its match in the Savior, it still for a time remains a threatening, menacing force. Near the close of the first century, the defeated but still active evil began to break forth in the form of a great persecution of the people of God. Notice how the Revelation describes this evil force: "And I saw a beast rising out of the sea. . ." (Rev. 13:1). But the final word in the final vision is a word of ultimate triumph: "Then I saw a new heaven and a new earth; for the first heaven and the first earth had passed away, *and the sea was no more*" (21:1). Evil, mortally crippled and defeated in the Christ event, had finally died and disappeared.

    2. *The End of the Curse.* The "original sin" not only brought disruption into the divine-human relation, but it also resulted in a "curse" being imposed on the natural world. "And to the man [the Lord God] said . . . cursed is the ground because of you; in toil you shall eat of it all the days of your life; thorns and thistles it shall bring forth for you; and you shall eat the plants of the field" (Gen. 3:17-18). Not only does this passage demonstrate the intimate relation between the human and the non-human creation, but it also emphasizes the devastating effect of sin, extending far beyond a simple act of disobedience.

In the third section of the book of Isaiah the prophet anticipates the time when the curse will be lifted and the joy, peace, justice, and harmony of the original earth and its inhabitants will be restored. God will create a "new heaven and a new earth." In that new creation "the wolf and the lamb shall feed together; the lion shall eat straw like the ox; but the serpent—its food shall be dust! They shall not hurt or destroy on all my holy mountain, says the Lord" (Isa. 65).

When Paul offers hope to those who suffer for Christ and are longing for future glory, he says that the creation also "waits with eager longing for the revealing of the children of God; for the creation was subjected to futility, not of its own will but by the will of the one who subjected it, in hope that the creation itself will be set free from its bondage to decay and will obtain the freedom of the glory of the children of God. We know that the whole creation has been groaning in labor pains until now" for redemption (Romans 8:19-22).

When John is given his vision of the culmination of the birth pangs of the new creation, he sees the result as a "new heaven and a new earth; for the first heaven and the first earth had passed away" (Rev. 21:1). The curse has been lifted and the original goodness of the creation has been restored. For this wonderful day the whole creation groans and waits.

3. The End of Profanity. The popular use of "profanity" as bad language will not help us here. We must remember that the Book of Revelation is profoundly informed by the Old Testament. It has even been suggested that the book is written in code and the code is the Old Testament. In fact, without an intimate knowledge of the Old Testament one cannot interpret Revelation properly. This final book of the Bible is a mosaic of allusions, quotations, and images taken from the Jewish Scriptures, and it interprets these in terms of the person of Christ. Thus, the Old Testament provides the concepts for John's vision of the final consummation.

In Israelite thinking, all of life was divided broadly into two compartments—the holy and the common (see Lev. 10:10-11). That which was common could be either clean, which was their normal state, or unclean because of ritual or moral defilement. Only that which was clean could be sanctified or set apart for sacred use. In this context, "profane" was a synonym for "common." It does not have a necessarily derogatory tone but simply means ordinary—no different from any other object or person in that category. Since all holiness comes from being rightly related to God, the "profane" (or common) becomes holy by being put in right relation to God. Nothing that is unclean can be in that sanctified relation.

In the light of these distinctions, those who are unclean because of moral defilement suffer eternal separation from the "new heaven and new earth." They are the "cowardly, the faithless, the polluted, the murderers, the fornicators, the sorcerers, the idolaters, and all liars, their place will be in the lake that burns with fire and sulfur, which is the second death" (21:7-8). The New Jerusalem itself cannot have anything or anyone unclean within its precincts: "Nothing unclean will enter it, nor anyone who practices abomination or falsehood, but only those who are written in the Lamb's book of life" (Rev. 21:27).

On the positive side, the *holy* city that John sees in his vision is the full and complete embodiment of holiness. Nothing is "ordinary" or "profane" in the priestly sense of the term. No longer will there be a distinction between the sacred and the secular. Zechariah's vision of the final day will be fulfilled: "On that day there shall be inscribed on the bells of the horses, 'Holy to the Lord.' And the cooking pots in the house of the Lord shall be as holy as the bowls in front of the altar; and every cooking pot in Jerusalem and Judah shall be sacred to the Lord of hosts, so that all who sacrifice may come and use them to boil the flesh of the sacrifice. And there shall no longer be traders [Canaanites] in the house of the Lord of hosts on that day" (Zech. 14:20-21).

4. *The Beginning of Eternal Earthly Life.* Perhaps most startling for popular Christianity is the fact that the saints are not caught up to heaven to exist forever in some disembodied state. Although the New Testament says almost nothing about heaven, it doubtless can best be viewed as a marker for the "intermediate state" of the saints awaiting the final resurrection. While not explicitly stated, New Testament faith knows nothing of the kind of eternity often envisioned by popular imagination. Rather, it speaks explicitly of an *embodied* immortality that follows the resurrection of the body. The New Jerusalem refers to the saints themselves more than to a place where the saints will live. Heaven can appear even now and will come even to earth.

REFLECTIONS

Have you ever wondered why the life of faith is often a struggle? We are constantly threatened by disease, disaster, and death. Both individually and collectively, the human race is faced with forces that seek to turn our world into chaos. As someone once put it, history is a slaughter-bench at which men are sacrificed by forces over which they have no control.

Today we are looking down the barrel of potential global annihilation. Weapons of mass destruction have the capacity to destroy the human race. Environmental decay bodes ill for planet earth. These sobering facts have altered the way recent generations have come to look at life. In the 1960's Bernhard Anderson described it this way:

> Spreading around the earth like the drifting fallout from a mighty nuclear bomb is a profoundly disturbing sense of disorder. Peoples from various nations, races, and cultural settings are beginning to experience an affinity for each other, not because they agree at the level of political or philosophical discourse but because at the depth of their being they share a common anguish in the face of radical uncertainty.[47]

The same general malaise is sensed strongly by the "millennials" (those born from the early 1980s to the nearly 2000s). Owning a home, a traditional symbol of long-term family stability, is no longer one of the important things in life. The deeply disturbing fact is that a large percentage of the new generation has not made any personal effort to help the environment. Why? It is not worth the bother since there is no real future anyway. Long-range plans seem futile. Time-honored values of permanent vocations and stable family life have been abandoned for short-term relationships. Who knows what the future holds?

One result of this dramatic new view of life is that many people have given up any faith in divine providence. They have come to affirm that the great questions of human existence have no firm answers. In fact, apart from momentary satisfactions, life itself is essentially meaningless. Evil is more real than good and apparently will triumph in the end.

It is easy enough to close our eyes to this situation and blithely declare, "God's in his heaven and all's right with the world." That is, it is easy enough until tragedy strikes our own life. The doctor diagnoses the sickness as cancer, our loved one is snatched away by some catastrophe, and things that only happen to other people come home to us. Then we begin to wonder what is going on, or maybe we even ask where God is? Or is there a God at all?

Some religions make their living by playing on these dimensions of life. They suggest cheap and easy answers and offer remedies that can best be described as escapism. Not so with biblical faith. It looks squarely into the face of the stark reality of the tragic aspects of life,

---

[47]Bernard Anderson, *Creation versus Chaos*, 11.

refuses to explain them away, and manages to affirm its faith anyway. The book of Revelation is all about this realism. It reminds us that all appearances to the contrary, Jesus Christ *has conquered evil* and in God's timing that victory will become eternally and finally complete if we do not lose our faith and collapse into unnecessary chaos and despair.

There is a grand vision to be seen with John from the mountain. Here is a beautiful summary of this vision for our lives in the waiting period:

> John lets his picture speak for itself. His language throughout this vision is indicative. "This is how it will be." And yet as always the indicatives of biblical theology contain an implicit imperative, the gift becomes an assignment. If this is where the world, under the sovereign grace of God, is finally going, then every thought, move, deed in some other direction is out of step with reality and is finally wasted. The picture does not attempt to answer speculative questions about the future; it is offered as an orientation for life in the present.[48]

Questions to Think About

1. What is the fallacy in attempting to use the Book of Revelation to predict history in advance?
2. How does Revelation illustrate the primary purpose of prophecy?
3. How is John's final vision an affirmation of the goodness of creation?
4. How doe the message of Revelation emphasize the centrality of Jesus in God's ultimate purpose for the world?

---

[48]M. Eugene Boring, *Revelation* in *Interpretation* (Louisville: John Knox Press, 1989), 224.

CONCLUSION

My wife and I, in our sunset years, have been blessed with the challenge of rearing our great granddaughter. At this writing she is nine years old and is a really bright light in our lives, as well as keeping us on the move. As I was working on this manuscript, her school was on mid-term break so we took her on vacation to the mountains in East Tennessee, a new experience for her. We wandered around the streets of the resort village of Gatlinburg--which was filled with tourists--past tourist trap after tourist trap. Some we fell for—and enjoyed. However, the experiences we were having of the marvelous natural phenomenon of the Smoky Mountains was myopic. Then this enthusiastic little girl decided she wanted to take a ride on the chair lift up the steep mountain nearby. So she and I did what I had previously been too chicken to try and discovered that it was worth the trip. As we rose up above the valley, and the panorama unfolded before us, the bustling tourists on the streets were left behind, the buildings that housed the offers of strange sights and sounds faded into insignificance and we could see it all in perspective. It had rained the night before and the clouds were still hovering around the peaks reminding me of how often the clouds had appeared in the mountain top experiences I had been exploring in the preceding pages. In a word, from the mountain height, we gained perspective.

The trek that we have been taking together, if you are still with me, has touched on most of those events that embody the biblical story. That story moved from the fallen predicament of humankind that initiated God's redemptive action, through his efforts to use a faulty people to bring about the restoration of his creative intention for the world and the human race, to finally sending his own Son as the "one faithful Israelite," who brought about a new order of being through his resurrection from the dead. From the vantage point of this history-altering event we scaled the mountains that gave us a vision of the final consummation of history in the coming of the Kingdom of God to earth in all its fullness. In a word, this series of mountain revelations gives us a view of the entire sweep of the biblical story.

We have been able to discern a definite pattern. All of those mountain top visions prior to the birth of Jesus demonstrated incompleteness. It was a story looking for an ending. The people who populated that story anticipated a future intervention in history that would finally answer the human longing for redemption from the slavery to sin. In this sense, we have seen that Jesus Christ is the consummation and crown of all Old Testament revelation. Although the presence of God was with his old covenant people, their repeated failures elicited the hope that the glory of God would some day come in a way that would transform them from within. John began his Gospel with the celebration that this hope had become actual when he declared that "the Word became flesh and lived among us, and we have seen his glory, the glory as of a father's only son, full of grace and truth" (John 1:14). A.M. Ramsey spoke movingly about that glory: "Insofar as [glory] means the power and character of God, the key to that power and character is found in what God has done in the events of the Gospel. In so far as [glory] is the divine splendour, Jesus Christ *is* that splendour. And in so far as a state of light and radiance awaits the Christian as his final destiny, that light and radiance draw their meaning from the presence and person of Christ."[49]

What we have seen in these visions from the mountain tops is the long history of Israel reaching its climax. It was a culmination that did not involve the abolishing the world and history, but its redemption. In a word, it involved a "new creation," the inauguration of a new order of being through Jesus' Resurrection. He did not return from the dead to the old order[50] but he passed through death to the other side, into this new order of being. Thus the Christ-event was the turning-point from which at last the long history of the world would change course.

We are living in a period of history in which the secular mind has deliberately set out to deny this radical implication. It has sought to impose its unbelief on all literary products by the use of different markers for the calendar. Now, we are told, we are living in the "common era" (C.E.) not the "year of our Lord" (A.D.) and the dividing point of history marks off the B.C. era as the B.C.E. (before the Common Era). If we understand the significance of the events of the work of Christ, we know that there is nothing "common" about the age in which we live. This transformation took place through real historical events that changed everything. It was not merely a new set of ideas, or a new religious experience but a world-transforming phenomenon,

---

[49] A.M. Ramsey, *The Glory of God and the Transfiguration of Christ* (London: Longmans, Green & Co., 1949), 28.

[50] This was doubtless the point of Jesus' word to Mary at the tomb not to "cling to him." She wanted him to be there as he was before but this was not to be.

although all this other was included. This truth means that there is a Christian worldview that stands over against all other worldviews.

What difference would it make if God had not sent his son "in the fullness of time?" I recently heard the answer to that question in a speech by a self-professed extreme right-wing Jewish agnostic who is a *New York Times* bestselling author. Demonstrating a quite good knowledge of the Old Testament, he argued that all "progressive" attempts to correct the injustices of human society are futile, and would fail, because human nature is evil, their permanent and unchanging condition being described in Genesis 1-11. Possibly unaware of it, he was articulating the Christian doctrine of "original sin" and using it to malign the assumption that had informed the social gospel of the 19th century and that he claimed informed contemporary progressive politicians. He seemed to forget that Christian analysts in the mid-twentieth century had already challenged that optimism on the basis of a renewed awareness of the depth of human depravity—remember Reinhold Niebuhr and his classic work on *The Nature and Destiny of Man*!

What was so fascinating was his repeated affirmation that the only hope for justice in this present age is "a divine intervention." What he apparently was not aware of, with his highly pessimistic secular worldview, was that such a "divine intervention" had already occurred. The entire world of people and nature was not transformed but the "new creation" was inaugurated and the door of possibility was opened through the work of Jesus Christ for a transformation of human persons. St. Paul celebrates this truth in the letter to the Romans as he describes how, in the death and resurrection of Jesus, the covenant faithfulness of God to his promises to Abraham came to a climax and in that event the power of the Holy Spirit was released for those who by faith became "children of Abraham" (justification) making it possible to experience victory over sin in this life. In the light of this confidence, the Apostle asks, "What shall we say then, shall we continue in sin that grace may abound?" and answered with a resounding "No." "For God has done what the law, weakened by the flesh, could not do: by sending his own Son in the likeness of sinful flesh, and to deal with sin, he condemned sin in the flesh." Now, in Christ, "you are not in the flesh: you are in the Spirit, since the Spirit of God dwells in you."

But Paul, with the rest of the New Testament, does not leave it there. The "new creation" inaugurated by the work of Christ will in God's timing reach a culmination in which the entire cosmos will experience "redemption." Paul speaks of this future glory in Romans 8:19-21—"For the creation waits with eager longing for the revealing of the children of God; for the creation was subjected to futility, not of his own will but by the will of the one who subjected it, in hope that the creation itself will be set free from its bondage to decay and will obtain the freedom of the glory of the children of God." When Jesus came out of the tomb, the new creation was launched. We are now living between Easter and the final consummation. Our assurance, as Paul says in Romans 8, is that the presence of the Holy Spirit is the guarantee, the earnest, that the Spirit that raised Jesus from the dead and dwells in our mortal bodies will also be the means of our final resurrection as well as the renewal of the cosmos in a "new heavens and new earth." In this light we should resonate with the response of Leslie Newbigen who, when asked if he was an optimist or a pessimist when he looked at the church in the modern world, responded, "I am neither an optimist nor a pessimist, Jesus Christ is risen from the dead."

APPENDIX – THE LAND

We have suggested that the most adequate way of characterizing the Hebrew-Christian scriptures is as a story that recounts God's dealings with human beings and their world from the creation to the consummation. The Old Testament phase of the story is largely played out on or in relation to a piece of real estate some 100 miles long and 50 miles wide between the Mediterranean Sea and the Arabian Desert. According to the covenant with Abraham (Genesis 12:1-3; 15) this land was promised to the patriarch and his descendents in perpetuity. In the New Testament phase of the story the theme of the land that plays such a major role in the Old basically drops out of the picture. What is the significance of this absence?

The issue raises questions of biblical interpretation, the relation between the Old Testament and the New, the nature of biblical prophecy and has even impacted political policy. The relationship between Israel and the "Promised Land" has become a major issue for many, if not the majority of, evangelical Christians. The issues involved are so widespread and complex that it could take a major research project to explore them with any degree of completeness. That is beyond the scope of this work but since the references to the land have appeared with such prominence in the studies of this book, it seems appropriate to provide at least a cursory comment about what I believe is a position consistent with the Christian faith.

There first needs to be a brief statement about the nature and purpose of God's gift of the land to Israel. It is rooted in two basic scriptural truths. First is the creation of human persons in the image of God. We have inferred in this work and fully developed elsewhere the idea derived exegetically that the image of God involves multiple relations including a relation of responsible stewardship of the earth. Many instructions in the Mosaic Law gave guidance how to carry out this mandate.

The second truth is the election of Israel as the descendents of Abraham to be the means through whom God will deal redemptively with the Adam problem. One major aspect of this purpose was to embody in their corporate and individual lives the image of God and thus be "the light of the world." In the light of these two truths it seems quite feasible to believe that the purpose of the gift of the land was so that Israel could demonstrate the mandate to care for the environment. It was to be a pilot project for new creation. However, in time, possession of the land seemed to have become an end in itself. This was likely present in Israel's self-consciousness from the beginning.

It is furthermore fundamental to recognize that inhabiting the land was conditional in nature. The emphasis on God as owner and Israel as a tenant presupposes this relationship. This relation is presupposed by the prohibition against selling the land (cf. Lev. 25:23). The Mosaic warnings in Deuteronomy put the conditional possession of the land beyond question (Dt. 28:1-3, 7, 10).

In the 19th century under the influence of a Calvinistic view of covenant, a movement emerged among the Plymouth Brethren that became known as Dispensationalism that systematized the idea of an unconditional covenant between Israel and the Lord. An aspect of this was an emphasis on the literal fulfillment of Old Testament prophecies and on the basis of this assumption developed a complete eschatology. This literalistic reading of the prophecies of the pre-exilic prophets appeared on the surface to support a high view of inspiration. That was part of its strength. The system of biblical interpretation was popularized by the Scofield Bible notes, a study bible that continues to be widely used among conservative Christians, although it has been revised.

As suggested one major aspect of this movement was a preoccupation with the prophecies of Jeremiah and Ezekiel. Both declared the inevitability of the expulsion of Israel from the land because of their sin but emphasized with equal clarity that God would subsequently bring Israel back to the land but that return would also include a spiritual transformation that would address the wayward hearts that each prophet recognized stood at the core of the problem.

These assumptions became the basis for an explosion of pop prophecy that surrounded the establishing of the state of Israel in 1948. This was exacerbated by the rise of the Zionist movement that claimed a divine basis for Israel possessing this particular piece of real estate. The International Christian Embassy said:

> We simply believe the Bible. And that Bible, which we understand has not been revoked, makes it quite clear that God has given this land as an eternal inheritance to the Jewish people. . . According to God's distribution of nations, the Land of Israel has been given to the Jewish People by God as an everlasting possession by an eternal covenant. The Jewish People have the absolute right to

possess and dwell in the Land, including Judea, Samaria, Gaza and the Golan.[51]

This perspective was evidently the assumption of Jesus' immediate followers even after his resurrection as reflected in their question to him upon his instruction to wait in Jerusalem for the gift of the Holy Spirit: "Will you at this time restore the kingdom to Israel (Acts 1:6). John Calvin wrote, "There are as many mistakes in the question as there are words."[52] And as contemporary evangelical John Stott noted in his commentary on Acts:

> The mistake they made was to misunderstand both the nature of the kingdom and the relation between the kingdom and the Spirit. Their question must have filled Jesus with dismay. Were they still so lacking in perception? . . . The verb, the noun and the adverb of their sentence all betray doctrinal confusion about the kingdom. For the verb *restore* shows they were expecting a political and territorial kingdom; the noun *Israel* that they were expecting a national kingdom; and the adverbial clause *at this time* that they were expecting its immediate establishment. In his reply (7-8) Jesus corrected their mistaken notions of the kingdom's nature, extent and arrival.[53]

In a lecture titled "The Theology of the Land," Stephen Sizer drew out the practical implications of the kingdom of God as inaugurated by Jesus:

> The kingdom which Jesus inaugurated would, in contrast to their narrow expectations, be spiritual in character, international in membership and gradual in expansion. And the expansion of this kingdom throughout the world would specifically require their exile from the land. They must turn their backs on Jerusalem and their hopes of ruling there with Jesus in order to fulfill their new role as ambassadors of his kingdom.

---

[51]Quoted by Stephen Sizer, "The Theology of the Land," online.
[52]*The Acts of the Apostles 1-13* (Edinburgh, St. Andrew's Press, 1965), 29.
[53]*The Message of Acts* (Leicester: Inter-Varsity Press, 1990), 40-41.

Behind this debate lies a long history of discussion about how Christians should read the Old Testament. The question is, how can the Old Testament be accepted as a Christian book? How can we justify the claim of the New Testament, especially St. Paul, that Jew and Gentile alike, and without distinction, are the children of Abraham, the one people of promise? Does this not deny that Israel is special? Is it not the source of anti-Semitism? These charges are regularly made. These are the issues that constituted one of the first theological struggles of the early church. And the church vigorously opposed the exclusion of the Old Testament from the Christian canon, like the position of Marcion, a second-century heretic who denied that the God revealed in Jesus was the same as the God of the Old Testament. One view is that the Apostles' Creed was composed to counter this interpretation.

The New Testament itself, of course, from start to finish sees the gospel of Jesus as the fulfillment of all that God had promised to his people in the Old. That was the point Jesus was making on the road to Emmaus when he explained to the two puzzled disciples all the things in the scriptures which concerned himself. This claim is the foundation of the Christian faith. One of the specific things on which the New Testament insists, again and again, is that in the life, death and supremely the resurrection of Jesus the promised new age has dawned. The return from exile has happened. "All the promises of God", says Paul in 2 Corinthians 1.20, "find their 'yes' in him." This is in fact the end of exile, even though it doesn't look like people had thought it would. Instead of Israel as a political entity emerging from political exile, we are invited in the gospel to see Israel-in-one-person, the true king, emerging from the exile of death itself into God's new day. That is the underlying rationale for the mission to the Gentiles: God has finally done for Jesus what he was going to do for Israel, so now it's time for the Gentiles to come in. That, too, is the underlying rationale for the abolition of the food laws and the holy status of the land of Israel: a new day has dawned in God's purposes, and the symbols of the previous day are put aside, not because they were a bad thing, now happily rejected, but because they were the appropriate preparatory stages in God's plan, and have now done their work. Lift up your eyes, says Paul in Romans 8, and see how the promises to Abraham are to be fulfilled: not simply by a single race coming eventually to possess a single holy strip of turf, but by the liberation of the whole cosmos, with the beneficiaries, the inheritors of the promise, being a great number from every race and tribe and tongue, baptized and believing in Jesus Christ and indwelt by his Spirit. Jesus, in the Sermon on the Mount (Matt. 5:5) had already pointed this out. Note the adaptation of Psalm 37:11.

> To suggest, therefore, that as Christians we should support the state of Israel because it is the fulfillment of prophecy is, in a quite radical way, to cut off the branch on which we are sitting. It is directly analogous to the mistake of the Galatians, who thought that if they were members of Abraham's family they should go the whole way and get circumcised. It is similar to the mistake of which the Reformers accused the mediaeval Catholics, of supposing that in every Mass they were actually re-crucifying Jesus, when Jesus' death had been once and for all, never to be repeated, on Calvary. It is a way of saying that in the cross and resurrection God did not actually fulfill his whole saving purpose; that Jesus did not in fact achieve the fulfillment of Old Testament prophecy; that his resurrection was not the start of God's new age; that Acts is wrong, Romans is wrong, Galatians is wrong, the letter to the Hebrews is wrong, Revelation is wrong. Say that if you like, but don't claim to be Christian in doing so.[54]

No wonder John Wick Bowman, in an analysis of the notes of the Scofield Study Bible, concluded that if Dispensationalism is not a heresy, nothing is a heresy.[55] But there is a biblical basis for Christian support of Israel. Paul himself highlights it in Romans 3:1-2. The ethnic descendents of Abraham were the ones who carried the redemptive line until it reached its culmination in Jesus. As the Apostle emphasizes, this does not mean that they were thereby excluded but may continue as part of God's chosen people by faith in Jesus. Nonetheless, the Jews

---

[54]The final section of this appendix, including the quote, is heavily dependent on N.T. Wright, "The Holy Land Today," (Originally published in *The Way of the Lord: Christian Pilgrimage in the Holy Land and Beyond*. 1999, London: SPCK; Grand Rapids: Eerdmans, 119-130. Found in www.ntwrightpage.com.

[55]"Dispensationalism," in *Interpretation*, April 1, 1956.

are the ones who were recipients of the faith that informs the Christian religion. After all, Jesus was a Jew.

Printed in Germany
by Amazon Distribution
GmbH, Leipzig